MACHIAVELLI

and

Renaissance Italy

is one of the volumes
in the
TEACH YOURSELF HISTORY
LIBRARY

Teach Yourself History

VOLUMES READY OR IN PREPARATION

The Use of History, by A. L. Rowse
Pericles and Athens, by A. R. Burn
Alexander the Great and the Hellenistic Empire, by A. R. Burn
Agricola and Roman Britain, by A. R. Burn
Constantine and the Conversion of Europe, by A. H. M. Jones
Charlemagne and Western Europe, by H. St. L. B. Moss
Wycliffe and the Beginnings of English Nonconformity, by K. B. McFarlane
Henry V and the Invasion of France, by E. F. Jacob
Joan of Arc and the Recovery of France, by Alice Buchan
Lorenzo dei Medici and Renaissance Italy, by C. M. Ady
Machiavelli and Renaissance Italy, by J. R. Hale
Erasmus and the Northern Renaissance, by Margaret Mann Phillips
Thomas Cromwell and the English Reformation, by A. G. Dickens
Cranmer and the English Reformation, by F. E. Hutchinson
Elizabeth I and the Unity of England, by J. Hurstfield
Whitgift and the English Church, by V. J. K. Brook
Raleigh and the British Empire, by D. B. Quinn
Richelieu and the French Monarchy, by C. V. Wedgwood
Oliver Cromwell and the Puritan Revolution, by Maurice Ashley
Milton and the English Mind, by F. E. Hutchinson
Louis XIV and the Greatness of France, by Maurice Ashley
Peter the Great and the Emergence of Russia, by B. H. Sumner
Chatham and the British Empire, by Sir Charles Grant Robertson
Cook and the Opening of the Pacific, by James A. Williamson
Catherine the Great and the Expansion of Russia, by Gladys Scott Thomson
Benjamin Franklin and the American People, by Esmond Wright
Warren Hastings and British India, by Penderel Moon
Washington and the American Revolution, by Esmond Wright
Robespierre and the French Revolution, by J. M. Thompson
Napoleon and the Awakening of Europe, by Felix Markham
Bolivar and the Independence of Spanish America, by J. B. Trend
Jefferson and American Democracy, by Max Beloff
Pushkin and Russian Literature, by Janko Lavrin
Marx, Proudhon and European Socialism, by J. Hampden Jackson
Abraham Lincoln and the United States, by K. C. Wheare
Napoleon III and the Second Empire, by J. P. T. Bury
Alexander II and the Modernisation of Russia, by W. E. Mosse
Gladstone and Liberalism, by J. L. Hammond and M. R. D. Foot
Livingstone and Africa, by Jack Simmons
Clemenceau and the Third Republic, by J. Hampden Jackson
Woodrow Wilson and American Liberalism, by E. M. Hugh-Jones
Lenin and the Russian Revolution, by Christopher Hill
Botha, Smuts and South Africa, by Basil Williams
Roosevelt and Modern America, by J. A. Woods

MACHIAVELLI

and

Renaissance Italy

by
J. R. HALE

THE ENGLISH UNIVERSITIES PRESS LTD
102 Newgate Street
LONDON, E.C.1

First Printed   .   .   1961

Copyright © 1961
J. R. Hale

PRINTED AND BOUND IN ENGLAND
FOR THE ENGLISH UNIVERSITIES PRESS LTD
BY HAZELL WATSON AND VINEY LTD, AYLESBURY

A General Introduction to the Series

THIS series has been undertaken in the conviction that there can be no subject of study more important than history. Great as have been the conquests of natural science in our time—such that many think of ours as a scientific age *par excellence*—it is even more urgent and necessary that advances should be made in the social sciences, if we are to gain control of the forces of nature loosed upon us. The bed out of which all the social sciences spring is history; there they find, in greater or lesser degree, subject-matter and material, verification or contradiction.

There is no end to what we can learn from history, if only we would, for it is coterminous with life. Its special field is the life of man in society, and at every point we can learn vicariously from the experience of others before us in history.

To take one point only—the understanding of politics: how can we hope to understand the world of affairs around us if we do not know how it came to be what it is? How to understand Germany or Soviet Russia, or the United States—or ourselves, without knowing something of their history?

There is no subject that is more useful, or indeed indispensable.

Some evidence of the growing awareness of this may be seen in the immense increase in the interest of the reading public in history, and the much larger place the subject has come to take in education in our time.

This series has been planned to meet the needs and

demands of a very wide public and of education—they are indeed the same. I am convinced that the most congenial, as well as the most concrete and practical, approach to history is the biographical, through the lives of the great men whose actions have been so much a part of history, and whose careers in turn have been so moulded and formed by events.

The key idea of this series, and what distinguishes it from any other that has appeared, is the intention by way of a biography of a great man to open up a significant historical theme; for example, Cromwell and the Puritan Revolution, or Lenin and the Russian Revolution.

My hope is, in the end, as the series fills out and completes itself, by a sufficient number of biographies to cover whole periods and subjects in that way. To give you the history of the United States, for example, or the British Empire or France, *via* a number of biographies of their leading historical figures.

That should be something new, as well as convenient and practical, in education.

I need hardly say that I am a strong believer in people with good academic standards writing once more for the general reading public, and of the public being given the best that the universities can provide. From this point of view this series is intended to bring the university into the homes of the people.

A. L. ROWSE.

ALL SOULS COLLEGE,
    OXFORD.

Contents

Maps

*To my colleagues
and pupils at
Cornell University
1959–60*

Preface

MACHIAVELLI'S books will be judged, as all books must be, on their own merits, but without a knowledge of the circumstances in which they were produced they cannot be properly understood. The reader of any of them must ask: What was its purpose? For what audience was it written? What sort of experience was the author drawing on? And the object of this book is to provide some sort of answer to these questions. For fourteen years, from 1498 to 1512, Machiavelli's career as an official of the Florentine chancery kept him in touch, during a period of almost constant crisis, with domestic politics, foreign affairs, and war, the themes of all his major works. Up to 1512, then—the year in which he was dismissed from office on the collapse of the republican government of Soderini and the return of the exiled Medici—we shall trace his acquisition of political experience; after that, we shall see under what conditions he expressed it in the series of works, *The Prince,* the *Discourses on Livy, The Art of War* and *The History of Florence,* for which he became famous. I am concerned only with the life of Machiavelli: not at all with his resurrection as Machiavel. The history of Machiavelli's reputation is an enthralling one, but it is best insulated from an account of the development of the man himself.[1]

I have not attempted to describe the political events of Machiavelli's youth. For this I refer my readers to

[1] The best introduction is still L. A. Burd's edition of *Il Principe,* pp. 31–69.

another book in this series, *Lorenzo dei Medici and Renaissance Italy,* by my late tutor, Dr. C. M. Ady, and my first acknowledgment must be to her for encouraging my interest in this period. The book to which I am most directly indebted is Roberto Ridolfi's *Vita di Niccolò Machiavelli,* Rome, 1954, by no means the longest but the most complete, relevant, accurate, sympathetic and wise of all lives of Machiavelli. My quotations from Machiavelli's dispatches are taken, sometimes in an amended form, from *The Writings of Niccolo Machiavelli,* vols. 3 and 4, by C. E. Detmold, N.Y., 1891. I am especially grateful to Dr. E. V. Rieu, general editor of Penguin Classics, for permission to quote from the new translation of *The Prince* by Mr. George Bull. I have received most valuable advice from Dr. Nicolai Rubinstein, and, while on a Fellowship at the Newberry Library, Chicago, from Dr. Hans Baron. I have greatly benefited from the vigilance of Professor F. O'Laughlin and Mr. Donald Carne-Ross.

I owe much on the score of encouragement, and of accuracy and coherence to this generous interest; for opinion and emphasis, however, I must bear full responsibility.

Finally, the style and sense of nearly every page has benefited from the trenchant and friendly criticism of Dr. A. L. Rowse.

J. R. H.

Cornell, May 1st, 1960.

CHAPTER ONE

Machiavelli: Some Preliminary Remarks

THE biographer of Machiavelli cannot complain that he is working in the dark, for his hero lived in a generation that observed itself with more energy and objectivity than any since classical times. The period from the invasion of Italy in 1494 by Charles VIII of France, when Machiavelli was twenty-four, to the savage sack of Rome by the troops of Charles V in 1527, the year of Machiavelli's death, wrenched the course of the peninsula's history so sharply from its track that contemporaries looked at their own world with the same amazed interest that an astronomer might show were the moon suddenly to reveal its back. France and Spain, formerly considered docile giants, weakened by domestic strife, were now seen as able and ruthless aggressors, with resources of men and money so great that wars to seize particular provinces in Italy developed into a struggle to decide which power was to dominate world politics, Valois or Habsberg. These wars involved defeats which led to much heartsearching among Italians: what has happened to our ancient valour? what has corrupted our strength? they asked themselves. The machinery of political change in Italy which had run slowly during the previous fifty years, when there was some degree of peaceful equilibrium between the greater states, Milan,

Venice, Florence, the Papacy, Naples, suddenly accelerated. States changed overlords not once but, in the extreme case of Milan, a dozen times. Others, while avoiding conquest, changed their constitutions, again not once, but repeatedly.[1] And within each short-lived system there were crises, some of which were surmounted while others developed into revolutions. Outside Florence, Machiavelli's home, old lessons were repeated in a more disturbing form : the danger to be feared from the greed of Venice, the least 'Italian' of the northern and central states; the danger of popes who were determined to use any weapon which would restore the temporal glory and security of the Church. And there were new lessons : the growing power of the Swiss, pressing down on the lip of the Lombard plain; the short-lived experiment of Cesare Borgia, who gathered a host of small semi-independent lordships into one centrally administered province in the Romagna. The crises of this generation provided a practical Anthology of Government and War, and no one with his eyes open could avoid reading it. To Machiavelli, a lover of the civilization that distinguished all the Italian states from the countries they called 'barbarian', a passionate Florentine patriot, a republican, and a professional civil servant, any war, any change of régime, was of direct personal concern. In 1512, indeed, failure of the Florentines to resist a 'barbarian'

[1] In the case of Florence, for instance, the government before 1492 was an oligarchy under Medici supremacy, after that, a more open one which failed. In 1494 she became a broad-based republic; in 1512 a narrowly based republic increasingly dominated by one family, the Medici; in 1527 a radical republic; in 1530 she returned, more effectively than ever, to the dominance of one family.

army led to a change of government and to his own dismissal.

These disasters fell upon the most articulate people in Europe. There was a strong tradition of historical writing. Family records were valued and personal journals kept. Diplomatic correspondence had trained a whole class of men to observe and analyse political events and personalities; commercial ramifications throughout the trading world had occasioned letters that kept families in intimacy as well as providing market reports. Nor was the scrutiny of events restricted to the surface. When the Florentines' independence had been threatened a century before by the expansionist policy of the despot Gian Galeazzo Visconti of Milan, their writers turned to history for encouraging analogies, and strengthened the resistance of their fellow citizens with studies in the meaning and history of republicanism. When Italy was struck by a far larger and far graver crisis, it is not to be wondered at that its mark was left on every form of literary record, from official histories to popular broadsheets and poems.

From literary sources and the records of government departments, then, we can know well, and at times intimately, both what happened in Italy and what men thought about it. Our information is especially complete for Florence, and in that most literate city Machiavelli was one of the most prolific writers of all. As a chancery secretary he was called upon to write thousands of routine letters; as organizer of the Florentine militia he wrote hundreds more; in the course of some thirty diplomatic missions he wrote enough dispatches to fill two stout volumes. He wrote, besides the brief *Prince,* three full-length books, the *Discourses* on Livy's Roman History, *The Art of War,* and *The History of Florence.* He wrote three plays and a short story. He wrote enough poems to fill a not-so-slim volume, and miscellaneous historical and political pieces enough to fill another. Lastly, we have over seventy of his private letters to friends, and more than twice that number of their letters to him.

Even the most routine official letter, passing on the decisions of his superiors, yields something about him, if no more than his whereabouts. The reports he was asked to draw up from time to time, in their blend of energy and academicism, reveal something of his temperament; the dispatches reveal still more. The literary works reflect his interests and the originality of his approach to them, and in the private correspondence the distance between his voice and the ear of posterity becomes narrowed to a surprising degree, for Machiavelli was one of the great letter-writers. To read one of his letters, a friend declared, was to hear him speaking, and if this is true it is easy to understand the charm his conversation had for men who, being better born or wealthier, would otherwise hardly have come to know him well. His main topics are scandal and politics, but the tone constantly varies from boredom and depression, on the one hand, to exhilaration and conviction on the other, now relaxed and desultory, now indulging in flights of fantasy or burlesque. Lyrical and ardent in one place, foul-mouthed and off-hand in another, sensitive, changeable, self-conscious: it is in these letters rather than in his measured works that Machiavelli comes near to convincing us of one of his favourite theses: that human nature always remains the same.

Yet with all this evidence to hand, something of Machiavelli's personality remains elusive. Style may be in part the man—and Machiavelli's, pungent and economical, was unmistakably his own—but if it is instinctive and flexible, it can hide as much as it reveals, and there are few passages in his letters where Machiavelli cannot be sensed watching himself being spontaneous. Moreover, there was some core of reserve, some disappointment or self-disgust, which Machiavelli did not choose to reveal. To divert attention from his heart, he painted a false one on his sleeve, and took pleasure in representing it as a bad one. If a friend described a disreputable adventure. Machiavelli would cap it with a worse. 'I never believe what I say, or say what I believe', he wrote on one occasion to a friend who knew very well how passionate and sincere his opinions could be. The crowded audiences of his play *Mandragola* were told in the prologue that the author was an aggrieved and malicious man who fawned on his betters. This dramatic exaggeration is another of Machiavelli's defences. To understand him it is essential to remember that he was the author of this play, the most vital comedy in the Italian language. The dramatist's eye for effect is to be found in his prose, here in a calculated overstatement, there in an abrupt change of tone, as it was in his everyday life. It was this sense of the dramatic that prompted him, when sent late in life on a trifling mission to a monastery at Carpi, to arrange that he should be sent armed messengers who would arrive in a sweat of urgency, with just enough energy left to slip from their horses and hand him bogus dispatches which he read through with a great show of importance while the friars clustered round in awed admiration.

A flair for the dramatic, coupled with a wry self-awareness; a temperament that allowed the fullest rein to intellectual enthusiasms while never fully releasing personal ones; this complexity, not rare but fascinating in Machiavelli's case because of the quality of his genius, can be read not unfairly into the sole portrait that has come down to us. It was painted by Santi di Tito, posthumously, but employing a death-mask, and certainly for close friends who could advise and guide the artist. (Machiavelli died out of favour; there is no question of a portrait commissioned by a conventional but indifferent public authority.) It shows a neat, spare man; the face has fairly high cheek-bones, a strong, rather large nose, a thin mouth, nearly smiling. The large black eyes look quizzical. His ears are set far back, dark hair brushed close to reveal the shape of the skull. His skin is pale. The figure's expression is a little wary, amused but withdrawn; an observer's face.

If Machiavelli was an onlooker in that he usually regarded events, and always himself, with detachment, he was at the same time an avid participator both in public affairs and private relationships. The books for which he is famous are the product of enforced idleness. He wrote *The Prince* in the year after his dismissal from office, and he would far rather have been writing up the minutes of government committees or recruiting reluctant peasants in the Tuscan countryside. Activity and companionship were the drugs he craved. When poverty and unemployment forced him to retire to the country and he was deprived of both, it is not surprising that, on turning to the study of Roman history, he saw its great men as figures to whom he could talk, and its crises as guides to action in current affairs. The study of antiquity was conventional enough in the Renaissance. Others studied it with greater scholarship, but none with a greater personal need.

In the graph of Machiavelli's life, the steep arc of youth is missing : we see only the flattened curve of maturity. The first genuinely revealing document is a letter written when he was nearly twenty-eight. We know something about his family, a few facts about his early schooling, but in an age when character was formed precociously, where a man might anticipate becoming a general at twenty, our understanding of Machiavelli's character is sadly hindered by this lack of early evidence.

We know enough about his family to be able to place him socially, an important matter in class-conscious Florence. His lawyer father represented an old country nobility become urban bourgeoisie, with a coat-of-arms, a little property but a small income, and he had married into a similar family. What he had worked at before 1498 we do not know, but in that year he gained a civil service post, responsible but subordinate, the sort of post conventionally filled by men of his background. From then until the disaster of 1512, he worked unceasingly and absorbedly.

The core of his job was the formulation and dispatch of instructions from the committee—the Ten of War—which handled war and foreign relations. Instructions to ambassadors went out over his signature,

as did orders to the mayors of country villages to provide labour or supplies when Florentine armies were in
the field. He was sent himself on diplomatic missions.
Though full ambassadors were men of high social
standing, men of lesser rank were often employed to
act as their secretaries, or brief them more effectively
than could be done by post, or to act independently on
missions of small importance; sometimes mandatories,
as they were called, were sent so that their action could,
in case of need, be disavowed by their employers. There
was no professional diplomatic caste; indeed, as many
government offices rotated every few months, government came to a large extent into the hands of amateurs.
Responsible men who were not part of the administration for the time being, however, could be chosen as
ambassadors, just as they could be summoned to attend
meetings of the more important advisory committees,
called *pratiche*. As a result, there were a few influential
men, of sufficient birth to impress foreign governments,
and enough wealth to supplement their meagre allow-
ances, who were practically full-time ambassadors. For
during the premonitory muttering of the storm, and
still more after its breaking in 1494, the Italian states
liked to keep more or less permanent representatives at
foreign courts, so that dangerous moves could be
anticipated, shaky alliances kept in repair. Such men
were received honourably by the aristocratic courts of
the north; two of them, during Machiavelli's period
of employment, were treated with great personal
friendliness by the king of France and allowed to join
the lilies to their own coats-of-arms.

In contrast, agents of an inferior order were com-
monly regarded as spies, tolerated because they were

accredited representatives of their government, but cold-shouldered by the court and forced to pester and bribe their way to information; it was they who saw the seamy side of international relations most clearly. Machiavelli as a permanent official who had a knowledge of all the diplomatic correspondence passing through his department was a natural choice as mandatory, and justified it by proving himself as welcome at foreign courts as an employee in his grade could well be. In the course of these missions he met and spoke with the rulers of France and Germany, Louis XII and Maximilian, with Pope Julius II and with Italian princes like Cesare Borgia and military leaders like Gaston de Foix. This diplomatic experience was decisive in shaping his political ideas. It enabled him to see Italy from the outside, to see the factious strife of the peninsula magnified into the terms of international politics, to watch and appraise the forces—rulers, their advisers and generals—who were remoulding, sometimes deliberately, sometimes almost casually, the destinies of the Italian states. In the prefaces to all his polemical works, *The Prince*, the *Discourses*, and *The Art of War*, he insists that his arguments are based on both classical precedent and modern experience. Few men, indeed, were better situated to study the political scene than Machiavelli, constantly engaged either in reading diplomatic correspondence or in writing it. To make analyses of political affairs that are subject to immediate proof or disproof by events is a useful training for any writer on political theory; to Machiavelli, who tended to be more interested in the pattern of an argument than in its practicability, it was of particular value.

The other concern of his department was war. Florence had no reliable army of her own—she hired professionals, who fought under their own leaders while Florence provided pay and saw to transport, victualling, the supply of ammunition and other stores. The armies were accompanied by Florentine commissaries, and, as in the case of diplomacy, these men were private citizens usually chosen from the most influential class : from among the *ottimati*, the *grandi*, the *uomini da bene*, to give the contemporary synonyms. These men did what they could to help the armies in the field, but they also acted as a political control on the military. Here again Machiavelli showed himself to be indispensable, first as go-between, then as commissary in all but name. His reliability and energy impressed Piero Soderini, head of the government from 1502, and he functioned increasingly as Soderini's personal aide. He was fascinated by the whole business of war, brooded on its theory, tirelessly mastered its details. He was responsible for persuading Florence to enroll its rural subjects in a militia which he organized, and his attention to the minutiae of supply and disposition in the final campaign against the important rebel city of Pisa were considered, at least by his friends, to have played an important part in Florence's victory. These successes deepened his interest. After 1512, he devoted as much space in his writings to war as to politics, and would possibly have preferred posterity to think of him as a military expert rather than as a political or constitutional theorist. Apart from *Mandragola* and the poem *The First Decade*, the only one of his books to be published during his lifetime was *The Art of War*.

As a result of his fourteen years' employment Machiavelli had talked with some of the world's rulers, he had made friends in a class above his own, among the *ottimati*, he had revolutionized the city's military resources. But this prosperity was not secure. It was in the nature of a wartime commission. In 1512, when he lost his government post on the return of the Medici from exile, he reverted, as it were, to civilian status. He retained his *ottimati* friends; indeed, he made more; but though they enjoyed his company and admired his talents, they were chary of pushing him forward for re-employment. At first matters were complicated by Machiavelli's identification with the Soderini family, now out of favour. But the Soderini became reconciled to the Medici, and many of his *ottimati* friends were restored to favour with them. Machiavelli remained excluded, and when he was eventually offered employment it was in the form of a trifling mission like the one to Carpi, or a contract to write a history : nothing that would bring him back to political life or assuage his thirst for participation in great events, even in a subordinate capacity. Possibly, too, as one bar to re-employment—the Soderini connection—lost its force, another took its place. Machiavelli became more eccentric, more incalculable, more rackety. This did nothing to spoil his welcome at dinners and literary groups, but it did complicate his admission to the sober Medici party machine. His reaction to adversity was such that while he became more acceptable as a companion he became less admissible as a colleague.

Machiavelli was one of those men of high nervous energy to whom the only balance to overwork is dis-

sipation. He could neither feel, nor act, by halves. Yet
at the same time there was some self-conscious inhibitor
at work that prevented his feelings from having their
free and natural play. He described this state of tension
himself in an undated poem :

> *I hope—and hoping feeds my pain.*
> *I weep—and weeping feeds my failing heart.*
> *I laugh—but the laughter does not pass within.*
> *I burn—but the burning makes no mark outside.*

To calm the distress caused by the failure of his
career and the ruin that threatened Italy and Forence,
Machiavelli could not call on the resources of religious
faith. This was just before the challenge of Protestan-
tism made men chary of criticizing their Church.
Machiavelli girded at the political conduct of popes
and lampooned hypocritical and lascivious friars, and
in this he was doing nothing unusual. His anti-cleri-
calism was hardly more violent than that of many of
his friends, including Francesco Guicciardini, who was
one of the Pope's senior officials. Where he differed
from most of them was in looking on religion as one of
the forces a politician has to take into account, important as an ingredient in the citizens' education. Used
well, Christianity could make a craven into a hero ;
used ill, it could soften a nation by teaching it to turn
the other cheek. He considered it on a par with other
religions : the irrational has to be taken into account,
whatever its label. He praised its reformers, like Moses
and St. Francis. He was concerned with its effect not on
the soul but on morale. As a result of this objectivity,
he was unable (as some of his friends, with spiritual
needs equally shallow and critical senses equally acid,

were not) to receive any comfort from the Church. His discussions of right and wrong in the political world betray the pressure of a nostalgia for a world where, if men were wise and moderate, God's will would serve as a guide in private and public actions alike. He used biblical illustrations in his works, at moments even of especial fervour, as in the last chapter of *The Prince*. He used phrases like 'May God guide things for the best', 'May God receive his soul', and ended letters to members of his family with 'Christ guard you' in a natural and conventional way, and such phrases became more common in his later years. When he was asked to write a homily on the theme of repentance to be delivered at a meeting of a religious confraternity, he did so simply and without his tongue in his cheek. But for all this, to Machiavelli the Christian faith, though providing a store of august or tender associations, had nothing personal to say.

His morals were similarly utilitarian. Sins of the flesh he comprehensively condoned. Sexual faithfulness was not considered by him, nor by his nearest friends, as a necessary part of marriage; infidelity impaired neither duty nor affection. But about sins of the purse he was positively puritan. Waste, unnecessary luxury, ostentation—these were signs of a corrupt citizenship, of men who spoiled the state to line their own pockets, and who put private comfort before public duty. Man's inclinations became wrong when they threatened the welfare of the state as a whole; a man must give up the luxury of obeying his private conscience if society as a whole would suffer as a result. His belief in the folly of striking fine moral attitudes at moments of desperate crisis was based on the conviction that they would find no answering gesture from the other side. It is folly to throw away your sword when other men are only hiding theirs. Capable of strong affection for both men and women and of something like hero-worship for a few individuals like Antonio Giacomini, who represented his ideal of bravery and civic self-sacrifice, Machiavelli's idea of human nature was nevertheless without illusions. Most men, he thought and observed, put self-interest first. 'Everyone', he says in the Prologue to his play *Clizia*, 'but most of all the young, thoroughly enjoys watching an old man's cupidity; a lover's frenzy; the tricks of a servant; the greed of a sponger; the misery of a poor man; the ambition of a rich one; the wiles of a harlot —and what little trust can be put in anyone.'

Such beliefs made him sardonic but allowed him to be gay. A general pessimism armed him to some extent against the defection of individuals. He continued to find pleasure in the company of men like Filippo Nerli, who did not really like him; the failure of a friend like Francesco Vettori to make an effort on his behalf when he sorely needed help was not allowed to interrupt the most varied and interesting correspondence of Machiavelli's life. He had qualities of wit, enthusiasm, and fantasy that kept him near the centre of a circle of friends, most of them better born, some better scholars—Machiavelli knew no Greek, and his missions abroad had only given him no more than a few words of French—and some of them lovers of the fine arts, which he, as far as we know, was not. In all his writings there is only one mention of a work of art: in the Introduction to the *Discourses* he laments that men study and cherish even the battered remains of an antique statue, but remain blind to the lessons of ancient history. But in the generation after the death of Lorenzo dei Medici, Florentines of the ruling and bureaucratic castes were more interested in politics than in painting, and nine out of every ten of Machiavelli's waking thoughts were concerned with politics: constitutional forms, foreign affairs, and war. These were his hobby-horses, and they appeared in nearly everything he wrote apart from the plays and one or two poems. Some, indeed, of the poems, like the two *Decades*, are directly concerned with politics, and especially interesting in this connection is *The Golden Ass*, which shows politics intruding into a romantic framework with almost ludicrous effect.

The Golden Ass is an unfinished poem of 1517–18 intended as a satire on contemporary society and using the story of Circe and her herd of men turned into animals as its setting. The first canto is autobiographical. Machiavelli compares himself to his hero, the ass : he no longer cares who attacks him, he is used to ingratitude, takes blows for granted—all this in reference to his continued neglect by the authorities. Then he tells the story of a young Florentine who suffered from a peculiar neurosis : he could not resist dashing down any open street he saw in front of him. His perturbed parents had him treated by doctor after doctor before finding one who managed to keep him quiet for more than a month. Then, one day, he was walking soberly along the via de' Martelli when he saw the via Larga stretching broad and spacious ahead ; his hair began to stand on end, his resistance broke, and he started to run wildly down the length of the street. So I, resumes Machiavelli, having been quiet and patient for a while, turn back to savage criticisms of the times.

The story then begins and tells how the poet was met in a forest by one of Circe's maidens who smuggled him into her mistress's palace on all fours, so that he could avoid his transformation into a beast for a time at least. The fourth canto describes his entertainment there. The maiden's charms, the initial shyness and consequent pleasure of the night that followed, are all described with accurate relish. Next morning—and in the next canto—the mood changes abruptly. The maiden leaves to tend her animals, telling him on no account to quit her room. As soon as he is alone, he begins to muse, to think of the past, of the role Fortune plays in man's affairs—within a few lines the poet is reviewing his few but obsessive interests, topics treated at large in the recently completed *Discourses*: Venice trusting too much in fortune and antagonizing her neighbours; Athens and Sparta ruined by expansion; the German cities saved by their moderation. He briefly considers Florence before moving on to yet other *Discourses* topics: virtue brings peace, peace idleness, idleness foments the causes of war; nothing remains long in one state, all is constant flux. And he ends by reflecting on the folly of nations who have trusted in prayer alone, necessary as this is to political hygiene. God does not help those who do not help themselves.

Unfinished and unpolished, *The Golden Ass* is perhaps the most revealing personal document we have apart from the private letters. The two cantos four and five are almost a parody of Machiavelli's two main interests, women and politics; they resemble the alter-

nate treatment of these themes in his correspondence
with Vettori : a letter of scandal and gossip followed
by one of current affairs. The story of the Florentine
youth nicely exemplifies Machiavelli's nervous dread
of inaction, and his promise to snap and savage—
paralleled by a similar sentiment in the *Mandragola*
prologue, written at the same period—points to a social
malice which would fit in with his temperament, but
which is nowhere explicit in his work, save in a lam-
poon on his ex-patron and friend Piero Soderini. Yet it
is impossible to think that this man with so sharp
an eye for the absurd and so exact a tongue for describing it, conscious of high talents and resentful at their
neglect, irritated by ineffectiveness, conscious, possibly,
of an obligation to be amusing, living in a city famous
for its critical spirit, should not have satirized his fellow
citizens. Being Machiavelli, he did it with a swingeing
brio, and among the prosperous rakehells who fre-
quented Donato del Corno's tavern where Machiavelli
spent much of his time when up from the country, and
among the patrician intellectuals of the Oricellari
gardens where he was a favoured guest, Machiavelli
may in this way have enhanced his reputation as a
brilliant talker while undermining that of being a 'safe'
man.

The study of ancient, particularly Roman, history
was familiar enough by Machiavelli's day; it was part
of the cult of the antique world which characterized
Italian culture since the days of Petrarch. Machiavelli
was not interested in knowledge for its own sake (he
considered becoming a teacher, it is true, but only for
a moment, in a mood of the blackest depression) and
for him the relevance of Roman politics and war was

as obvious as a knowledge of ancient medicine to a doctor or sculpture to an artist. Ancient Rome seemed alive, not only because she was, after all, the direct ancestor of contemporary Italy, but because Machiavelli had learned a Latin that enabled him to read Livy as easily as he read Dante. Indeed, Roman writers spoke directly, without the archaisms that emphasized historical distance in the vernacular. It was as natural for Machiavelli to feel at ease with the heroes of Livy as for Petrarch to have written a letter to Cicero. Machiavelli read fairly widely (over twenty classical authors were used in the *Discourses*) and took care to be accurate in his facts and quotations, but his attitude towards classical literature was less that of a scholar, weighing evidence and comparing texts to find out exactly what happened, than of a politician searching for maxims and examples with which to lard his speeches. And apart from a taste for Latin chapter headings, Machiavelli had no scholarly affectations; he neither wrote his private letters in Latin nor filled them with Latin tags. Apart from some conventional formulas, the business of his department was conducted largely in Italian; he spoke Latin abroad, but we have no evidence that he could have composed literary Latin if he had wanted to. He provided in the contract which he himself drew up for writing *The History of Florence* that it might be done either in Latin or the vernacular, but he had no doubt; that work, like all his work, was the product of a mind that thought in concrete and sinewy Tuscan, and had urgent things to say. It is not that he was seeking a popular audience. The Florentines were prouder of their Italian than were other states of theirs; there was something fusty, mannered, or playful if a non-academic topic were served up in Latin instead of in the tongue shaped by Dante, Petrarch, and Boccaccio. He wrote for a small known audience. The international currency of Latin did not concern him. He wrote his books, as he had written his official reports, as though he were arguing them in person to a group of associates.

Though much of his writing was done, perforce, in retirement, Machiavelli was eager to discuss his work and to seek advice. None of his literary interests cut him off from other men, with whom, indeed, they were shared. Biagio Buonaccorsi, his closest friend in the chancery, wrote a history of Florence during his own years of chancery employment; Guicciardini had written a history of Florence while Machiavelli was still in office and was to write the most famous of all histories of Italy after his death; Vettori, too, wrote a history of his own times. Two other members of the Oricellari circle, Filippo Nerli and Iacopo Nardi, became famous historians of contemporary affairs. Both these men, and Guicciardini, shared Machiavelli's interest in constitutional adjustments. While few of his friends in Florence actually wrote plays they took a keen interest in them. Vettori's *Travels in Germany* included a play he claimed to have seen there, and in at least one of the anecdotes that fill that dreary work there is a marked resemblance to the story of *Mandragola,* a play Guicciardini much admired, and planned to have performed in Faenza under his auspices as governor. Of his other friends, Cosimo Rucellai, owner of the Oricellari gardens, was a poet, and another, Luigi Alamanni, was both a poet and a dramatist. Machiavelli was secluded by nothing but poverty. Though he was suspected of being in the middle of one conspiracy and on the fringe of another, there was nothing of the conspiratorial or the surreptitious about his interests or his actions. He was not a revolutionary in that sense, nor, in spite of his core of reserve, was he a solitary.

He shared the interests of his times, just as, to a large extent, he shared their values. He lived in a city of factions, where the word 'liberty' almost always had some selfish connotation. International relations were dominated by rulers, monarchs, and popes, whose word held just so long as their interests were maintained. Central Italy, where, Machiavelli thought, as did many beside him, some degree of consolidation was essential if Italy were to be strong, was lawless and brutalized, where poisonings were commonplace and vendettas could run to cannibalism. As a Florentine, he had grown up to think sourly of fine words; even Savonarola, with whose republican ideas he was in sympathy, he thought to be personally time-serving and ambitious. As an Italian, he lived his whole mature life in an atmosphere of war or warlike crisis, where political strategy was a dither of expedients and where weakness forbade the fine gesture or noble risk.

Like his fellow citizens, he felt involved with the *provincia*, with Italy as a whole, the cultural unit that continued the traditions of Rome and was thus superior to the barbarian races who had received this revelation only at second-hand; but his real love was for the *patria*, for Florence. Italy as an abstraction was much bandied about during these wars with the barbarians; it was shouted as a war-cry in battle, and a figure of *Italia* was painted in the office of the Florentine war department, where Machiavelli worked. But Florence had rejoiced when Naples had been conquered by the French in 1501, rejoiced again in 1507 when they occupied Genoa and came to an agreement with Spain to crush Venice, and gloated when that agreement brought Venice to her knees two years later. For Florence was concerned, more than with any other, broader issue, with the recovery of Pisa, in revolt against her from 1495 and only regained in 1509. For support in this undertaking she relied on the help of France, while other Italian powers, Milan and especially Venice, tried to prevent its success. A general resentment against Venice as the most recently powerful of the Italian states was exacerbated by this particular local issue, and prevented Florentines from feeling anything but political antipathy for her, though her constitution was admired for its stability, and there were personal links of friendship between the two states. Machiavelli was a bitter, almost an extreme, critic of Venice as a political power, yet he was no doubt pleased by the enthusiastic reception given to his *Mandragola* when it was performed there.

The failure of the Italian states to unite was due in part to antipathies of this sort, in part to a failure to grasp the enormous resources of the transalpine powers ; each withdrawal, it was felt, would be the last. The degree to which a central Italian could misconceive his city's relative importance to the world in general is strikingly illustrated by a comment of the Perugian chronicler Maturanzio on a faction brawl in 1495 : 'And men reasoned of this thing not only in Tuscany but over the whole of Italy, nay even in Muscovy, as I am well assured, and in other distant regions.' But even states with reasonably good intelligence services failed to see that after each withdrawal France and Spain could return with larger armies than before. Besides, each foreign army needed allies in Italy so there were always some native elements that stood to gain. The common people disliked the foreigners as individuals, because strange soldiers meant loss to farm and family; but Italian society was cosmopolitan and adopted some of their manners and fashions even while fighting them.

From this blur of sympathies and antipathies—mixed feelings for one another, mixed feelings about the foreign invaders—no sentiment of national unity could grow. The most that was thought of was a temporary league to protect the independence of the peninsula and so allow its states to pursue their own ways once the danger had passed. Commenting on a remark in Machiavelli's *Discourses* to the effect that the papacy had prevented Italy from ever having been governed by one king, Guicciardini pointed out that this was just as well; diversity suited the Italian temperament. In the last chapter of *The Prince*, Machiavelli urged the need for consolidation and the sinking of differences under one leader. He persuaded himself in this moment of enthusiasm that some semblance of united action might be imposed for a while from above, but he had no illusions about anything more fundamental. Indeed, in the same year in which he wrote *The Prince* his reply to a suggestion of Vettori's that Italy might be saved by a united front was a flat 'You make me laugh'.

When he shared so much, it might well be asked where his originality lay. Largely it lay in his approach. In his *Decades* he transformed the rhymed chronicle by incorporating shrewd judgments on men and affairs and general reflections on politics, so that they still live, although each line is briskly packed into its *terza rima* bed as by a nurse rather than by a mistress. In the *Mandragola* we still recognize how much Renaissance comedy owed to Plautus and Terence, but it is the first play to use their influences as a springboard rather than a prop; it is the only Italian play of this period with vigour, characterization, and style enough to hold the stage today. In a history-writing age, his *History of Florence* was unique. Breaking from the old-fashioned annal and diverging from fashionable humanistic historiography, he produced a work which was at once realistic, because it dealt with men as political animals and showed them at their intrigues, and also didactic, because he manipulated those events in the past which he thought had the most relevance to the present with such gusto that their lessons could not be missed. If this involved distortion, he was not concerned; the present is more important than the past. Because of its formal resemblance to old manuals *Of Princely Government*, Machiavelli's *Prince* was like a bomb in a prayer-book; while the *Discourses* transformed a commentary on a classical text into a constitutionalist's *vade mecum*. *The Art of War* was the most comprehensive work of its sort and the first that saw war as a continuation of political activity. 'You have always been *ut plurimum* at odds with the conventional, and an inventor of new and unexpected things', wrote Guicciardini in 1521. There is a chaffing note in this; Guicciardini was too cautious and settled a personality to let it be quite a compliment. But it was true. Even in the slight *Dialogue on our Language* there is a twist of novelty when he suggests that it is by the use of the verb that languages are best to be distinguished. Machiavelli touched nothing which he did not transform.

His choice of the part of speech which gives to prose its vigour and speed was a suitable one, for Machiavelli's style, spare and strong, would have brought him fame for its own sake. He is among the very greatest writers of Italian prose, if not the greatest of all, with a style which has the pungency of the colloquial without its slackness, and which, full of an energy of its own which might threaten to draw its author from the precise expression of what he had intended to say, is always the twin of his thought. Shadowing his mood from banter to gravity, from lucid exposition to urgent appeal, it can best be compared to his own ideal of the statesman : a man balanced always on the balls of his feet ; poised to spring whichever way opportunity should prompt.

It was an age that brooded much about free will: not in a theological but in a personal and political sense. When Opportunity appeared, represented as dashing past with flying forelock and the back of her head so bald that the man who clutched too late would find nothing to grasp, how far was man free to try to seize her, how far was he bound by the nod or frown of Fortune ? Writers too sophisticated to bring in God as the explanation for surprising events and not yet possessing historical method enough to fill the vacuum, invoked Fortune instead. In worldly hands, in Guicciardini's, for instance, fortune was little more than a code word for the myriad little unforseeable, incalculable circumstances that lie between a decision and the act. In other hands fortune became more of a God-substitute, in fact a goddess, the Fortuna of the ancients. It was against this tendency that the Counter-Reformation moved when it censored references to *fortuna* in Castiglione's *The Courtier* and substituted more off-hand words like 'chance' instead.

Machiavelli's preoccupation with fortune began during his long attendance on Cesare Borgia in 1502, when he saw that in politics, where events were in a state of flux and so many men were hesitant, the reso-lute ruler stood the best chance of success. He used the term in different senses, but, in the main, his treatment of fortune is characteristically energetic. He feared lest the rulers of Italy, dazed with adversity, should yield themselves to fatalism, and drift with, instead of resist-ing, events. He admits that certain things, like illness, are beyond human control, and can endanger plans as they did Cesare Borgia's, who was ill at the vital moment of his father's death and the consequent papal election; but in *The Prince* he likened fortune to a flooded river which can be tamed by dams and dykes, and to a woman who can be shaken into submission if a man is resolute enough.

This feeling that the course of events could be changed was fundamental to Machiavelli's thought. It underlay the blunt extremism of the pieces of advice he drafted from time to time as a government em-ployee; it underlay the obsessive zeal he showed in the organization of the militia; it explains his search of the past for examples to spur and guide the present. He was aware that in political life there are so many contin-gencies that it is difficult to see the way ahead. Time after time in his diplomatic correspondence he admitted that he was baffled, that the future was anyone's guess. With so many contradictory surface phenomena, there was all the more need to cleave down to the general principles below them. There were constants: human nature was one; the fact that similar situations recurred throughout history was another. Study could find them out. This was the consolation of the years of retirement after 1512 when his work on Roman history and on the Florentine past enabled him to confirm and elaborate principles he had already determined on during his active years. It was only a partial consolation. To put those principles into effect leaders were needed, and armies, and Italy to all intents and purposes had neither. As a Florentine, he could give advice through *The Prince* and the *Discourses*, but as an Italian he was forced helplessly to watch the destruction of the peninsula by France and Spain. This is the mood of his last correspondence with Guicciardini; the theorist, with his useless knowledge of fundamentals, watching the incalculable trivia that will bring, sooner or later, the end.

There is something tiresome about the man who knows the answers, but does not have to put them into effect. And in Machiavelli there is more than a trace of the arm-chair pundit, a trait ridiculed, but with affection, by the *novella* writer Bandello. He describes how Machiavelli, famous as a military author but who had never actually led a soldier into action, was asked one day by Giovanni delle Bande Nere, the famous condottiere, if he would like to try out with his troops some of the formations described in *The Art of War*. Machiavelli leaped at the chance, but speedily reduced the ranks to a state of confusion from which he tried to

extricate them in vain. Giovanni let him flounder for
some time, then, as the day was hot and the hour for
dinner near, took over the command and in a few
minutes produced the movements his guest had
planned.

Yet though Machiavelli spent many heavy years
in retirement, he never looked on himself as 'retired';
he continued to hope for re-employment; he never re-
treated into the pursuit of learning for its own sake, or
indulged in reflection that would never have to bear
the test of events, or at least, discussion. His knack of
epigram, his confident tone, his taste for ingenuity, his
optimism—these tendencies had produced from the
beginning generalizations that were too rash, schemes
that were too fine-drawn to be thoroughly practical.
But he did not start as a man of affairs and dwindle
into a scholar. Writing when the government of
Florence was alternating between various forms of
republican and princely rule, it was impossible to write
in the abstract; every project was seen in the light of
a possible practical change of parties and personalities.
Before 1512 his ideas were shaped by the pressure of
events; thereafter they were shaped by the pressure
with which he forced himself to be in touch with
events, and with friends who were still involved with
them. For this reason, his ideas cannot be properly
understood in isolation: we must know the story of
his life.

CHAPTER TWO

The First Lessons: 1469 – 1500

———————

MACHIAVELLI was born on May 3rd, 1469. It was
the year in which Lorenzo dei Medici, later known as
the Magnificent, came to power on the death of his
father Piero. The Machiavelli, uninfluential as they
now were, nonetheless came from the Tuscan nobility.
They owned country property in the Val di Pesa and
some houses in Florence. Machiavelli's father, Bernardo, belonged to a branch of the family somewhat
less prosperous than the rest, and he needed what he
earned as a lawyer to keep his family of four children.
Machiavelli had two sisters, Primavera and Margherita,
who were nearly five and nearly ten years older than
himself, and a brother Totto, who was five years younger. They lived in what is now 16, via Guicciardini.

His mother may have been a woman of some culture; we know at least that she composed some religious poems. Bernardo, not greatly successful as a
lawyer—he left an estate cumbered with small debts—
was quietly bookish. He kept a bare matter-of-fact
diary of jottings that concerned his family and his
business and recorded the accumulation of a small
library. It consisted chiefly of classical texts the most
important of which, perhaps, was the *Roman History*
of Livy, a work that was to be the subject of his son's
longest work, the *Discourses*. It is significant both of

Bernardo's tastes and his income that his copy was a gift from the printer in return for compiling an index to the edition. The diary also notes the early stages of the young Machiavelli's education : Latin grammar at seven, arithmetic at eleven; an ordinary unspecialized education, mainly based on the Latin which was essential for the law, the Church, or the civil service. An entry for 1481 notes that the boy was doing Latin composition. After that, till 1498, the documents are almost silent. That Machiavelli remained at home can be inferred from a poem he wrote to Bernardo when his father was staying at his small property near San Casciano, Machiavelli's future home in the country south of Florence ; an affectionate poem, though fumbling and obscure in technique. In December 1497 he wrote on behalf of the family to press their claims over the living of a church in the Mugello against the Pazzi, who were also laying claim to it.

It was a period of great changes, and we know of his reactions to none of them. He was twenty-two when Lorenzo died ; twenty-five when the invasion of Charles VIII led to the flight of Lorenzo's son Piero and the creation, largely at the instigation of Savonarola, of a liberal republican constitution ; twenty-seven when Florence began her long, costly, passionate struggle to regain the rebel port of Pisa. The French had left Italy in 1495 ; thenceforward Florentine interests were divided between the war with Pisa and the decline in Savonarola's power.

That in 1494 the opinion of a friar should have dominated one of the most critical and civilized cities in Europe was a complex phenomenon. Under the evergreen protection of the Medici, no rival power

could grow up freely to take its place; the crisis came
with neither an individual nor a matured party interest
able to meet it. Savonarola had already made a profound impression on all classes. His uncanny flair for
accurate prophecy had astonished everyone: Lorenzo
had died, Innocent VIII had died, Charles had come,
Piero had fled, all as he had foreseen. His eloquence,
the rigour of the sacrifices he demanded, the ecstatic
confidence he showed in his mission to herald impending changes of vast moment: these qualities gained
him the support of those with strong, if conventional,
religious impulses, and of a large, if temporary, corps
of sensation seekers. But Florentine sophisticates, too,
were intrigued—in their case by his learning, with its
fashionable Platonic cast, and his emphasis on spiritual
regeneration, a process they, too, were hoping to aid
by their studies of divine inspiration in works previous
to or outside the main Christian tradition. He was out-
spokenly anti-Medicean and, though a Ferrarese,
flattered the Florentines by identifying himself with
them absolutely. In declaring for a republic and in
proclaiming Christ ruler of Florence, he ministered to
the two main needs of the moment—liberty and
prestige.

During the next three years, however, an inevitable
reaction took place. While on the one hand the appeal
of mortification began to wear thin, on the other, party
strife, confused under the Medici, began to sort itself
out. Savonarola soon found himself faced by three
main factions. One was the anti-austerity party, and it
included many clericals. Another was a group of
Medici supporters. A third, all the more dangerous for
not being sharply distinguished from the others, was

composed of men from important families who resented the inefficiency of the administration, and the
effect of Florence's political isolation—for she remained faithful to the unpopular French alliance—on
their peninsular trading and banking connections.
Their hand was especially strengthened when Savonarola's outspokenness brought about a breach with the
papacy. On March 9th, 1498, Alexander VI wrote to
the Florentine government saying that the friar was
excommunicated and must be listened to no longer.

On the same day, Machiavelli wrote about Savonarola to a friend, Ricciardo Becchi. It was a sharply
critical letter, showing that he judged Savonarola
purely from a political point of view, that he was
already detached from, and slightly contemptuous of,
religious enthusiasm, and that he was interested not in
spiritual experience but in rational argument. He
described two sermons. In one, Savonarola, fearful that
the newly elected signoria—many of the chief offices
in the state changed hands every two months—would
take the Pope's part against him, tried to rally his own
supporters by castigating the rival parties, and by
warning Florence that he alone stood between them
and tyranny. By the time he preached the second, the
new signoria had proved favourable to him, and as a
result he did not try to align his friends against his
enemies, but to rouse all Florentines against the Pope.
No more was said about tyranny. Pointing out the conflict between his attitude on these two occasions,
Machiavelli concluded 'and so in my opinion, he trims
with the times, and colours his lies to suit them'.

His dislike of Savonarola must have been well
known, for he owed his first—as far as we know it was

the first—job to it. The friar had misjudged the new
signoria; it was not prepared to support him against
the rising tide of unpopularity. Nine days later he
preached the last sermon of his life. On May 23rd he
was hanged and his body burned. His fall was followed
by a purge of his supporters, and Machiavelli, who
had already been nominated for a post in February
without success, was elected on June 19th to office as
Second Chancellor.[1]

The title reflects an earlier division of the chancery
of the Florentine government into two parts, the first
dealing with foreign, the second with internal, affairs.
Chancery officials did not make policy decisions, but
saw that the decisions of others were put into effect;
their offices were not subject to rotation, therefore, and
they were secure in all circumstances save a revolution
of the sort that had lost Machiavelli's predecessor his
post. The chanceries were run by six secretaries, subordinate to the First Chancellor of the republic, Marcello Virgilio Adriani, who was a friend, and possibly
patron, of Machiavelli. As Second Chancellor he was
automatically one of the secretaries, and ranked among
them in order of seniority of election. The secretaries
could be moved about among the government departments : in July Machiavelli was delegated to the Ten
of War (*Dieci di Balia*), the body that controlled
diplomacy and possessed authority which sometimes
overlapped that of the signoria itself; they could be
transferred to new bodies, as Machiavelli was in 1507
to the Nine of the Militia (*Nove di Milizia*) which or-

---

[1] I am following, in this section, an article by Nicolai Rubinstein, 'The beginnings of Machiavelli's Career in the Florentine
Chancery', in *Italian Studies*, 1956.

ganized the peasant army, or to temporary ones. In each case the secretary's job was to deal with the paper work of the department, pass on its orders and see that they were carried out, and provide an element of continuity among executives who came and went every few months. But they were not restricted to office work. Machiavelli was sent on missions abroad and elsewhere in Italy, as we have seen, by the Ten, and much of his work for the Nine was travelling up and down the Florentine dominions, recruiting and organizing units of the militia. The post, though subordinate, was a responsible and confidential one (*Secretarius* implied access to state secrets). It involved being close to the wider business of government; the duties were varied and the chancery itself was a pleasant environment. He found his colleagues congenial and speedily became firm friends with two of them—Biagio Buonaccorsi and Agostino Vespucci. Both of these men had literary interests—it was, indeed, a tradition in the chancery— and Adriani himself was a professor at the university and continued for a while to teach there while he was First Chancellor.

Florence was passing through a period of crumbling imperialism, trying to retain territories that were intent on freeing themselves and finding in foreign intervention added opportunities to do so. Pisa remained the main problem. This city, subject to Florence in the previous century, had offered itself to Charles VIII in 1494, and he had agreed to protect its citizens; it was the strongest card in his hand to play against Florence if she showed any signs of swerving from her alliance with him, but he promised to withdraw his protection when his Italian campaign was over, and, according to

his treaty with Piero dei Medici he had to hand back to
Florence the other fortresses he was keeping as pledge
of Florentine good behaviour. These were Sarzana and
Pietrasanta, controlling the coast road from La Spezia
south, and Livorno (Leghorn) on the same road south
of Pisa. These were the concessions that had settled the
fate of Piero.

After their conquest of Naples, the French returned
and were back at Pisa in June 1495. Here such earnest
and heart-rending appeals were made to Charles not to
throw them back on the mercy of the Florentines
that he undertook to preserve their independence and
left a French governor there when he moved on north.
This man, d'Entragues, identified himself completely
with the Pisan point of view, partly, it was believed in
Florence, because he had fallen in love there; he not
only refused to restore the city to Florence, but sold
Sarzana to Genoa and Pietrasanta to Lucca, rivals of
Florence. The Florentines recovered Livorno, it is true,
but it did not compare in value with Pisa as an outlet
for Florentine trade. Matters came to a head when in
January 1496 d'Entragues handed over the citadel in
Pisa to the inhabitants. That ended any possibility of
negotiation. Pisa could only be won back by war, and
any power that wished to hurt Florence could do so by
aiding Pisa, by sending reinforcements or creating
diversionary attacks against other parts of Tuscany.

The Pisan war, which occupied, on and off, the next
thirteen years, held a place in the concern of Florentines, and space in their history, that has seemed ex-
cessive to some, appearing, as it does, a side-issue in the
gravest international conflict since the Hundred Years
War. It bulks large, for instance, in Guicciardini's

History of Italy, and, according to Macaulay, 'there was, it is said, a criminal in Italy who was suffered to make his choice between Guicciardini and the galleys. He chose the history. But the war of Pisa was too much for him. He changed his mind and went to the oar.' The motives behind the war were part profit and part prestige. Pisa was Florence's wealthiest possession. It had been won after a hard struggle, and most of Florence's leading families had invested money in the city or in the surrounding countryside, and relied on its facilities as a port. Florentine money had been spent on amenities as well: its university was a Medici foundation. The customs figures do not allow a clear picture of the degree to which Florentine trade depended on Pisa at the end of the fifteenth century, probably less than at the beginning,[1] but in an age where land transport was so disproportionately dearer than water traffic, Pisa was still of prime importance. Silting of the mouth of the Arno had led to Porto Pisano being used more than Pisa itself by sea-going vessels, but goods were brought up through Pisa, and without Pisa the other was useless. The war was extremely expensive. Each spring operations recommenced, professional soldiers were hired, food and munitions procured. Extreme measures were taken; Pisan crops were destroyed, and attempts were made to foment discord within the city by making the poorer citizens resent the suffering forced on them by their aristocratic masters, and by tempting the peasantry to revolt from the urban domination that was costing them harvest after harvest. All this, for thirteen costly years, was of no avail. There was a continual leak of

[1] Information from Mr. Michael Mallett.

men and supplies into the city, and foreign aid helped to repair each winter the damage done in the preceding campaigning season. The Pisan antipathy for being ruled to the advantage of Florence was profound, and not only the men, but the women and children helped to repair breaches in the walls on the rare occasions when storming was imminent; occasions which were rare because the Florentines, though spending copiously on the war, were not prepared to make the sacrifices necessary to bring the war to a definite conclusion. It was always hoped that half-measures would somehow suffice. With hired troops, moreover, the returns were seldom proportionate to the outlay.

When Machiavelli came into office the Florentines were advancing under the condottiere general Paolo Vitelli, who took Vicopisano and Librafatta, and then, within a few miles of Pisa itself, called a halt, thus giving rise to some suspicion of double-dealing in the minds of his civilian employers, always touchy lest a condottiere might be receiving pay from both sides. This delay was all the more provoking since they had gone to the expense of hiring Ottaviano Riario, of Forlì, to guard against a diversionary attack from Venice, and while he was inactive in the east, Vitelli was doing nothing in the west. In September, however, the Venetian attack on Tuscany came: an army under the command of their condottiere the Duke of Urbino penetrated the Mugello and the Casentino. Vitelli's force was transferred from Florence, and held them off till winter brought the campaign to a standstill. Next April an agreement was reached between Florence and Venice through the arbitration of the Duke of Ferrara. Venice withdrew her troops, and

Florence was free to resume operations against Pisa. There were two main preoccupations at this point; a reappraisal of the strategy to be employed, and the procuring of enough mercenary troops. Machiavelli, inexperienced as he was, was closely concerned in both.

Some time between the agreement of April 16th and the reopening of hostilities in June, Machiavelli drew up a *Report on the Pisan War*. It does not represent Machiavelli's own original views; he merely conflates the views of the military leaders. You can take Pisa either by love or by force, he somewhat academically points out. Love is out of the question. It must be by force. Force could consist of blockade or storming, and after discussing the pros and cons of both, he concludes that the most economic and effective solution would be a combination : blockade followed by an assault. This report may be only one survivor of many such documents, and it is important to note that Machiavelli's powers of analysis were first exercised on military matters, where the either . . . or . . . fashion of argument, which was temperamentally congenial to him in any case, was perfectly suitable, or at least less misleadingly clear-cut than when used in discussing statecraft. The *Report* has a crisp and confident ring. Machiavelli was clearly in a position that suited him.

In March he had been sent to Iacopo d'Appiano, Lord of Piombino, who had asked for an increase in his pay as condottiere. In July he went on a more important mission to Caterina Sforza, ruler of Imola and Forlì, about the re-engagement of her son Ottaviano Riario, whose contract had expired at the end of June. Florence was interested in his troops, but still more in his mother's friendship; for her domains,

though small, were of considerable strategic importance, commanding as they did the approach to
Tuscany from the north-east, the direction of Venice.

It was characteristic of Caterina that she should do
the negotiating on her son's behalf. After Savonarola,
she was probably the strongest character Machiavelli
had yet encountered. Blunt, ruthless and imperious, at
thirty-six she was the survivor of three husbands, two
of whom had been assassinated, and she had learned to
bargain in a stern school. She lost no time in pointing
out that Ludovico Sforza was also competing for her
troops, fearing France as he did, and that Florence
ought first to pay over the debts that were still outstanding. Machiavelli wrote to the Ten from Forlì on
July 18th. 'I replied to the best of my ability, but could
not help observing that mere words and arguments
will not go far in satisfying her Excellency, unless
backed up, in part at least, by deeds.' A merchant-like
reluctance to part with money until the last possible
moment was a notorious characteristic of Florentine
statecraft. Machiavelli had censured this failing in his
Pisan report, but there he was probably recording the
experience of others, here he is voicing his own.

The countess kept him dangling for a few days,
while Machiavelli tried to estimate the chances of success. His dispatches were read with praise in the chancery, as Buonaccorsi told him, and this news, in spite
of Buonaccorsi's tendency to hero-worship his more
volatile colleague, was probably true, though events
were to show that Machiavelli could analyse a situation
better than he could conclude a deal. At one point the
countess agreed with the Florentine conditions of re-
engagement at a lower fee. Machiavelli wrote home to

this effect. Next day she blandly informed him that she had changed her mind. On this note the mission ended. But if he had lost the contract, Machiavelli had maintained the friendship the countess felt for Florence. Caterina wanted money; Florence security beyond the Mugello. Both were, in fact, quite satisfied.

Buonaccorsi, in his letters, had spoken of the progress made in the Pisan campaign and his longing for Machiavelli's return to help deal with the mass of business caused by an impending assault on the city. Machiavelli returned on August 1st. The auspices for a speedy victory were good. No other power was interfering, the besieging army was large, and Vitelli, its commander, was one of the most famous captains of the day. As his artillery pounded the wall, concentrating on the south-west corner of the city, some of the Pisans fled north to Lucca, and according to a contemporary, if the gates had been freely opened, Pisa would have been emptied of its population. Every ablebodied person was toiling to repair the breaches, but the guns were beating down more than could be replaced. On the 10th the Stampace tower was stormed, and the van of the assault penetrated the city near the Porta a Mare. It seemed a golden opportunity to second them. A long section of the wall was demolished, the army was full of confidence. The Florentine commissioners were in favour of pushing forward, so were the individual captains. But their commander was not. As the men came thrusting forward to pour through the breach, he and his brother Vitellozzo, stood in the way and with shouts and even with blows ordered them to withdraw. Their cries of 'Back! Back!' were received with bewilderment and grudgingly obeyed.

There were no more assaults. Next day Vitelli ordered the artillery to begin their work again, but the troops remained inactive. The news was received in Florence with amazement that rapidly hardened into suspicion, but for a while the Ten tried to humour Vitelli into making a second attempt. On the 15th they wrote—probably through Machiavelli—to urge him to try again. They referred flatteringly to his noble qualities, and anxiously to the speed with which time was passing. The whole letter was polite, but expressed a painfully restrained impatience. In conclusion they said that victory over Pisa would be hailed with admiration, not only in Florence and Italy but 'by the whole world', and that Vitelli would become famous, 'second to no other famous captain, even those of antiquity'. This attempt to flatter their general's vanity had no effect. They wrote to the Florentine army commissioners expressing despair at his extravagance and hesitations. He was using more ammunition than half Italy could supply, they complained on the 18th. On the 20th they reported with exasperation that 'we have had today letters from Milan to say that the French have taken by storm Annone, a well-fortified castle, strongly situated, well supplied with munitions, well garrisoned, *in one day*, and we have been twenty days over this siege, and the issue is still in doubt'.

At last their patience wore out. The commissioners were ordered to arrest Vitelli and bring him back to Florence for questioning. This was not an easy task. He was surrounded by his own men and his brother's, but on September 28th they brought it off with the same trick Cesare Borgia was to use at Senigallia, that 'finest of stratagems' for which he was so praised by

Machiavelli. The commissioners, with an escort, called on Vitelli in the morning to talk over the military situation with him, and after lunch, on the plea that the time had come to discuss more confidential matters, they retired to a room where they would be more private, made him prisoner and hurried him from the camp. In Florence he was tortured, tried, and, on October 1st, executed. The pious bourgeois, Luca Landucci, recorded in his diary that Vitelli was beheaded on the roof of the Palazzo della Signoria, 'the piazza being full of people. It was expected that his head would be thrown down into the piazza. It was not thrown down, however, but it was stuck on a spear and shown . . . with a lighted torch beside it, so that it could be seen by everyone. Then the people dispersed, considering that justice had been done, to the great honour of the city.' It was a popular verdict, but there were some doubts about its being a just one.

It is necessary to dwell on the Vitelli affair because Machiavelli for the rest of his life was haunted by the dangers of waging war with mercenary troops. This *cause célèbre* came at the beginning of his public career, and he was at the heart of it, conversant even with the highly secret negotiations that led to Vitelli's abduction. The case illustrates the difficulties facing the civilian employer of professional soldiers very clearly. The government looked on the fiasco from a political point of view. Vitelli had been in French pay before the Pisan war began, and there were still some French soldiers in Pisa. Was it collusion? During the previous winter he had obtained for the Duke of Urbino a safe-conduct out of the war zone on the plea of sickness. To please the Duke's employer, Venice? Dur-

ing August and September there was fighting in Lombardy between the new French king, Louis XII, and
Ludovico Sforza. Had Vitelli been waiting to see its
outcome? The case againset Vitelli was never proved.
There were no letters to show conspiracy, nor did he
confess to any, even under torture. All his actions could
be explained in terms of military courtesy or necessity.
His reputation, moreover, and therefore his income,
depended on success, on pleasing his employers. As the
government received more and more evidence of the
despondent state of mind of the Pisans on August 10th
—they had even been choosing ambassadors to sue for
peace—they became increasingly convinced of Vitelli's
guilt. But he, ignorant of this, might have made a
justifiable decision from a narrowly military point of
view—or did he think that the city might have been
stormed, but at a greater cost to his own men than he
was prepared to incur? These issues were clouded with
prejudices. Vitelli was impatient of political meddling
with the soldier's trade, and had been brusque to the
commissioners and indifferent to their demands. The
trial took place in an atmosphere of mounting hysteria.
Several of the commissioners had died of fever in camp
during the period of inactivity after the 10th. The prize
lost was not just any city, it was Pisa. The people were
anxious for blood, the government for vengeance on
the man who had mocked them both in pocket and
prestige. With the defiance of the weak, Florence was
showing that she was not to be trifled with.

Machiavelli believed in Vitelli's guilt. He had seen
how indifferently men fight for other men's causes and,
in the case of the Pisans, how devotedly in the defence
of their own. The Vitelli affair confirmed, if it did not

create, two of his life's dominant themes—the superiority of native soldiers to mercenaries, and the need for strong government action.

If August and September had been months of exasperation for Florence, they were months of anguish for Milan. By September 11th the French army, led by Giangiacomo Trivulzio, entered the city and Ludovico fled to Germany. In October Louis himself arrived, and was swiftly approached by Florentine ambassadors seeking his aid against Pisa. To this he agreed, in return for help in his expedition against Naples—whence the French garrisons had been expelled shortly after Charles VIII's withdrawal. But Florence soon saw the disadvantages of dealing with an ally whose interests were far wider than her own. Louis was also interested in gaining papal support, and in exchange for this he guaranteed to help Cesare Borgia, the son of Alexander VI, in his attempt to win back towns traditionally subject to the Pope but with a long record of independent rule. Among these were Rimini and Pesaro, ports on the Adriatic; Urbino, inland but covering the routes from Ancona—the most important port of entry from the east for Florentine trade—to Tuscany; and Imola, Faenza and Forlì, towns about whose custody, as we have seen, Florence was extremely sensitive. The first towns attacked by Cesare Borgia were, in fact, Imola and Forlì, the first of which fell in November, the second in December, though the countess held out heroically for another month in its castle; so to set against French aid in the Pisan war was the fact that French aid had changed these Romagnol towns from a bulwark to a threat. France, moreover, was insisting on the payment of loans made

for the Pisan war by Ludovico, and to argue the un-
reasonableness of this, an agent was chosen to negotiate
with the king's governor in Milan, Trivulzio.

The choice fell on Machiavelli. This would have
been his most responsible mission to date if it had
materialized, but while the French had been dunning
Florence they had been milking the Milanese still more
drastically, and when Ludovico made a reappearance
with a Swiss army, there was so much relieved support
for him that the French withdrew and Machiavelli's
commission was cancelled. This was in February 1500.

> *But swifter than I make these words to flow,*
> *In less time than you take to say 'Behold!'*
> *The Cock advanced in strength upon his foe.*[1]

In April a French army including Swiss troops advanced to meet him. Ludovico's Swiss refused—one of
the quirks of the mercenary business—to fight against
their own countrymen, and Ludovico was recognised as
he tried to file through the French camp disguised as a
foot soldier like the rest, and taken prisoner. It was the
end of his hopes. He died ten years later, still a captive
in France.

No sooner were the French back in Milan than Florentine ambassadors reminded them of the October
agreement. The French, firmer in the saddle now,
drove a shrewd bargain, though the Florentines were
allowed to choose their own general. They chose de
Beaumont, not for a military but, characteristically, for
a political reason : he had faithfully handed over
Livorno to them at a time when d'Entragues was hold-
ing on to Pisa. The greater part of the French aid con-

---

[1] *First Decade*, lines 253–5.

sisted of Swiss and Gascon mercenaries, men whose independent behaviour towards their original employer, man of war as he was himself, boded ill for their civilian sub-contractors.

Once under way, the behaviour of these troops was appalling. Factious and disobedient, constantly complaining about their provisions, they had no sense of responsibility towards the merchant-employers to whom they had been lent. They took Pietrasanta and then refused to hand it over. Within a few days they were on the verge of mutiny. Knowing their mood, Florence sent two supplementary commissioners to meet the army and march with it to Pisa, smoothing its troubles by the way. Machiavelli went with them as secretary. They met the army at Camaiore and accompanied it to Cascina—where its tumultuous behaviour prompted one of them, Luca degli Albizzi, to date one of his letters *Ex terribilibus Gallorum castris*—and thence to Pisa, where it sat down against the Spiagge and Calcisana gates and began to bombard the walls.

At one point enough of the wall was dismantled for an attack to be mounted, but this was called off when it was seen that the Pisans had prepared new defences inside the breach, and then confusions began which caused memories of this campaign to be even blacker than those of the last. On July 7th all the Gascons deserted. On the 8th the Swiss forced their way into Albizzi's room and demanded more pay. On the 9th Machiavelli wrote a dispatch to Florence marked Most Urgent to say that the mutinous troops had taken Albizzi prisoner. Five hundred Swiss had turned up uninvited, and Albizzi had been asked to pay them, which he refused to do, though to save his life he was later forced to agree. Most of the Swiss then marched off. The Florentines sent new commissioners, Piero Vespucci and Francesco della Casa, to conduct an inquiry at the depleted camp, and Louis sent an agent for the same purpose. Meanwhile, the Pisans sallied out, took Librafatta and the strong-points built in the previous year, and reopened communications with Lucca. The French agent offered more troops, but Florence called off the campaign in disgust.

Louis was furious at this turn of events. A detachment of the all-conquering French army had been sent

> *But left again in something near to flight*
> *And stained with scandal. So the truth was out:*
> *That even Frenchmen can be put to flight.*[1]

Threatening Florence with reprisals, he claimed that this scandal to French arms was due to their faulty handling of the campaign, especially to their grudging and inadequate provisioning of the army. There was enough justice in this charge to sting and force an answer. The Pisans, for instance, had been able to retake strong-points like the Ventura bastion because, though its commander had asked repeatedly for munitions, certain members of the Florentine government were using war money to pay themselves back for loans made to the city on previous occasions, and in this way private interest was competing with that of the public.

Somehow Florence had to talk her way out of this breach with her only ally. Two men were sent who had been concerned with the affair at first hand, Francesco della Casa and Machiavelli.

[1] *First Decade,* lines 277–9.

CHAPTER THREE

Four Formative Years : 1500 – 1503

IF Machiavelli's military ideas were influenced by his Pisan experience in 1498 and 1499, his political ideas were affected even more strongly by his diplomatic experience from 1500 to 1503, when he went to the courts of Louis XII, Cesare Borgia, and Julius II. Of all his life, these were the most formative years.

We have seen that chancery employees were used for minor diplomatic tasks or as subordinates in major ones. As mandatories they were not used to negotiate peace or war or marriage, but to explain, report, act as ambassadorial stop-gaps, and generally fill the blank spaces on a board where the chief pieces moved with magnificent deliberation. Ambassadors proper were wealthy men like Pierfilippo Pandolfini, who had entertained Charles VIII in his villa outside Florence in 1494, or Alessandro Nasi, round whose neck Louis XII himself placed a jewelled collar when the time came for him to leave the French court in 1508. Machiavelli's colleague, Francesco della Casa, was not of this standing, but he was experienced—he had already been to France on a mission for Piero in 1493—and came of a moderately influential family. As Machiavelli's senior in age and experience, he was in charge of the mission, but both men received similar pay.

In their commission of July 18th 1500, they were

ordered to make contact with the Florentine ambassadors already in France, and go with them to the king to explain the Pisan fiasco. 'The whole of this matter consists of two parts, viz : first, to complain of the disturbances which took place, and to make known their cause and the names of their originators ; and secondly, to defend and excuse us from any charge that might be levelled at us.' The chief causes of the trouble the government felt to have been partly the lack of control of de Beaumont over the troops, partly the intrigues carried on with the Pisans by the Swiss, and by members of the Trivulzi and Pallavicini families who, though nominally supporters of France, were known to have friends in Pisa. In making these accusations, considerable tact would have to be employed. With regard, for instance, to de Beaumont, the commission pointed out that 'although we have refrained from blaming the commander, not wishing to incur his enmity, nevertheless, when speaking before His Majesty the King, or other personages of importance, you have a chance of successfully laying the blame upon him, you will do so energetically, and must not hesitate to charge him with cowardice and corruption. . . . But until such an opportunity occurs, you must speak of him in an honourable manner and throw all the blame on others.' They were to be especially careful not to abuse him in front of the Cardinal d'Amboise, the most important figure at court and believed to be friendly to Florence.

Machiavelli and della Casa hoped to find the king—whose court was peripatetic—at Lyons, but he had gone when they arrived. The Florentine ambassador, Lorenzo Lenzi, was there, however, on his way home, and he briefed them on the best way to present their case. Even with Louis they should be tactful about de Beaumont; 'You must say that the trouble arose from his not having influence enough in camp, and from the natural gentleness of his character, which caused him not to be feared as much as he should have been.' As for the Italian traitors, they could be abused to the French, but should be flattered personally, especially as Giangiacomo da Trivulzio was influential at court. Machiavelli and della Casa reported to the Ten that they had met Lenzi, and that he had coached them and approved their arguments.

They then set off in pursuit of the court, which proved elusive, as it changed its course at every report of plague in the villages ahead. After some days of riding, Machiavelli wrote a personal letter to the Ten —the formal dispatches, though written out by Machiavelli, were concocted and signed together—to complain about his shortage of money. Machiavelli's salary was deducted from his mandatory's pay, while della Casa, who was not a government employee, had the whole of his available; the result was that Machiavelli had less money to spend during the mission, and 'It seems to me', he wrote, 'beyond all human and divine reason that I should not have the same emoluments. If the expenses which I incur seem to your Lordships too great, then I would observe that they are quite as useful as those of Francesco's, or the twenty ducats allowed me per month are simply thrown away. If in your opinion the latter is the case, then I beg your Lordships to recall me.' This tart missive was signed 'Humilissimus servitor, Niccolò Machiavelli'.

On August 7th they found the court at Nevers. They hastened to d'Amboise, primed with arguments in defence of their city's role in the Pisan affair, only to be told that the business was already half forgotten and of little importance. They then went to the king, but were again frustrated to see at his side not only d'Amboise but Giangiacomo Trivulzio and two members of the Pallavicini family. To complete their confusion the king at once admitted the bad behaviour of the Swiss and Gascons, and pointed out that de Beaumont was to blame for not having acted firmly enough. Against this last point, though it was one of their own, the Florentines had to protest, as it was made in the presence of d'Amboise. Their embarrassment was completed when Louis quickly dismissed the whole subject of their mission as out of date and asked what were Florence's intentions for the future; a question on which Machiavelli and della Casa had no instructions. They replied, tentatively, that if France were to take Pisa for Florence, then there would be no difficulty about payment in full for all her services.

While they waited for instructions from home, it was sharply born in upon Machiavelli how little Florence was respected outside Italy. On August 11th, when the court was at Montargis, della Casa and he had an interview with d'Amboise in which their arguments were contemptuously ignored. With regard to the Swiss, Machiavelli suggested that Florence was not bound to pay troops which had done nothing to earn it. 'To which the Cardinal replied that your Lordships ought to pay them, for if you did not, the King would have to do so with his own means, which would make him greatly dissatisfied with your conduct.' Machiavelli then said that the Florentines were greatly discouraged

by France's failure to restore Pietrasanta to her, after
which the conversation ran on these lines :

D'Amboise: France has promised Lucca not to do
this till Pisa has fallen.

Machiavelli: This is why—though you do not grant
this—the Lucchese are determined to prolong the war
with Pisa. And besides, the French are bound by their
prior treaty with Florence.

D'Amboise: All of his Majesty's obligations will be
fulfilled, provided your government does its duty in first
recovering Pisa. If it does not, then the king will hold
you responsible.[1]

Without instructions from Florence, too short of
money to buy useful information, della Casa and
Machiavelli hung on with uneasy feeling that the suits
of other embassies were prospering better than theirs.
Clustering for French favours were Lucchese and
Pisans, against Florence ; Venetians, against the Turks ;
Neapolitan exiles, against the current régime at home ;
papal agents, for aid to Cesare Borgia in the Romagna.
The only relief came in light-hearted letters from
Buonaccorsi, giving news and chancery gossip, and
saying how much he was basking in the admiration
caused by his friend's dispatches.

What the two envoys needed was not admiration
but instructions : news of some definite policy proposed
by Florence, preferably a generous one. Among the
criticisms of Florence made to Machiavelli by influential men at the court, two were especially galling because partly true : that Florence never won the game
because she was always counting the cost, and that she
could not be trusted because internal divisions made

[1] Paraphrased from Machiavelli's dispatch.

her irresolute. This was the price Florence paid for being a republic; it meant that to some extent internal liberty was bought at the cost of weakness in external affairs.

Machiavelli and della Casa, indeed, were treated with less and less respect. While their government tried to make up its mind, they repeated the old excuses until d'Amboise, concealing his impatience no longer, 'replied that these were mere words, and that they had no confidence in all our arguments, and was in short extremely dissatisfied with your Lordships. And this was said by him so loud that all the bystanders could hear it; and then he got straight on his horse to follow his pleasure.' Machiavelli wrote on August 27th to emphasize the folly of neither agreeing to pay the Swiss nor sending fresh ambassadors to show that Florence was prepared to take the initiative in reopening the war with Pisa. 'Nor must your Lordships imagine that well-digested letters or arguments will be of service in the matter, for they are not even listened to. *They are blinded by their power and their immediate advantage, and have consideration only for those who are either well armed or who are prepared to pay.*' This was the real world; money and arms were the only arguments that counted. As a weak state, Florence must be realistic; fair words and neat arguments were no longer of use. Because Florence was not armed, the French despised her. He bitterly recorded the gibe : 'They call you Mr. Nothing' (*Ser Nihilo*).

The weeks passed and still Florence made no move. Totto was nagging at the Signoria about Machiavelli's pay with no result. Machiavelli and della Casa were living in a penury as galling to their own pride as the continual criticism of Florence was to their patriotism. By September 26th, with della Casa away ill, Machiavelli wrote to say that he had taken it on himself to imply that ambassadors were on their way, his own rank, and that of della Casa, not being sufficient to keep the respect of the French. He repeated this hopeful fiction until d'Amboise commented cuttingly : 'So you have said, indeed, but we shall be dead before the ambassadors come.'

Machiavelli was not continually subdued by these vexations. He remained an intrigued observer of the political scene, and sometimes commented on it with what might have seemed to his government a provoking detachment.[1] 'I want to see now', he wrote on October 11th, 'how they will behave towards your Lordships; how they will use the money they demand of your Lordships, . . . how in case you declare yourselves their enemies, they will act so as to render you harmless.' He was resilient enough to send letters to his chancery colleagues which did much to raise their spirits. He had, indeed, plenty of time for observation and for letter-writing. Time passed and Florence made no move. Ambassadors arrived from Mantua, from Ferrara, from Naples. 'They all have more fear of this King than faith in each other,' Machiavelli commented, touching one of the root principles of contemporary Italian politics, the cause of much of the turning and twisting between alliance and betrayal.

During October Cesare Borgia followed up the cam-

---

[1] This point is made by G. A. Brucker in an unpublished Oxford B.Litt. Thesis, *The Diplomatic Career of Machiavelli*, which he was kind enough to let me see.

paign which had given him Imola and Forlì with another which yielded Pesaro and Rimini. The danger to
Florence was all the greater because he was being aided
both by the Pope and by France—still Florence's
nominal ally. On this theme Machiavelli had a conversation with d'Amboise to which he later referred in
chapter three of *The Prince*. He had heard that attempts were being made to poison Louis's mind against
Florence, especially by Alexander VI, who was pro-
posing that France should reinstate Piero dei Medici.
'Upon hearing all this, which seemed to me a plot
worthy of our Most Holy Father the Pope, I resolved to
say something to his Eminence of Amboise on the subject.' Louis, Machiavelli said to the cardinal, should
not trust those who were trying to alienate him from
Florence in order to further not France's but their own
ends. If he did, he would end by losing Italy altogether.
'His Majesty ought to prevent this by adopting the
practice of sovereigns who wish to establish and safeguard their power in a foreign country ; namely : to
weaken the powerful, conciliate the subjected, sustain
their friends, and beware of associates—that is, those
who want to exercise an equal share of power'—Venice
and the Papacy. Throughout this analysis, he concluded, 'His Eminence heard me patiently.'

But Machiavelli was not so absorbed in political observation at one of the hubs of international intrigue
that he preferred staying there to returning to Florence.
With the death of his father in May (his mother had
died in 1496), Machiavelli had become the head of the
family. His sisters were both married, and one died
while he was away in France. On October 25th he
wrote asking for relief on these family grounds. 'My

private affairs are so unsettled and without order, that my property is going to waste in every way.' The long-promised embassy was still hanging fire and Machiavelli was not back in Florence until January 14th, 1501.

In contrast to the previous months, this was to be a year of continuous activity. Machiavelli had not yet met Cesare Borgia, but he began to live in his shadow as he looked more and more truculently across Tuscany from his strong-points on the via Emilia. In April he took Faenza, midway between Imola and Forlì, and was created Duke of Romagna by the Pope. In May, after a move against Bologna, also a papal city but firmly and quietly ruled by the Bentivoglio family, from which he was warned off by Louis, he turned against Florence, demanding the return of Piero dei Medici, in whose hands Florence would become his most deeply committed ally. Taking Brisighella, key to the Val di Lamone route into the Mugello, he came on as far as Campi, between Prato and Florence itself, where he demanded a change of government and a condottiere's contract for himself.

To cope with this crisis, Florence made what military preparation she could, calling up irregular troops from the countryside and quartering them in the hills round the city. These men, raised temporarily and on a basis of one man per house, were not the sort of troops to put the city's mind at rest, and the citizens were divided between contempt for their government's pusillanimity—especially when the pistol-point demand for a contract was accepted—and fear for their own skins. With the contract and a safe conduct in his pocket, Cesare then marched contemptuously across

Tuscany, burning and terrorizing as though in enemy territory, towards Piombino, which he left his men to besiege while he himself withdrew to join the French army's march on Naples.

Machiavelli, less canny in this respect than his Venetian opposite number at the French court, had not realized how strong was Louis's determination to reconquer Naples, although the secret treaty of Grenada, for the partition of Naples between Louis and Ferdinand of Spain, had been negotiated while he was in France. By August, the campaign was over as far as the French were concerned, and the Neapolitan ruler, Frederick, resigned his kingdom and returned to France, the second Italian ruler to end his days there. The Spaniards under Gonsalvo of Cordova continued operations south of Naples, which ended in the following spring with the fall of Taranto and the capitulation of the duke of Calabria. The duke was given leave to retire to France to join Frederick, but the Spanish general sent him instead a prisoner to Spain—'neither the fear of God, nor care for the good opinion of men outweighing *raison d'état* (l'interesse dello Stato)', Guicciardini commented.

In the autumn of 1501 Machiavelli married Marietta Corsini but probably had little time to relish domestic life. It was a period of great uneasiness. With the fall of Piombino, Florence, with no troops in her employ, was caught between Borgian conquests, and the Pisans had offered to make Cesare their hereditary doge if he would bring them Livorno and save them from the Florentines. Louis was offended by the little support he had been given on his Neapolitan expedition and made much of Giuliano dei Medici, Piero's

brother, during a visit he made to France. Machiavelli
had been sent three times, in February, July, and
October, to try to negotiate a *modus vivendi* in Pistoia,
divided at that time by party feud and an easy prey to
any enemy who chose to walk up to her walls. But his
main concern had been with organizing the ramshackle
military forces of the republic during the summer, and
with arranging for the passage of the French army
across Tuscany in June.

Florence was more rent than ever by those divisions
for which the French had reproached her. In February
of the following year, 1502, it was clear that there were
mixed feelings about the French alliance itself, and the
policy of facing both ways, which Machiavelli had seen
might easily lead to complete isolation, was followed
to almost academic lengths. The emperor Maximilian
sent ambassadors to complain of Florence's supporting
France when the Empire was traditionally the power
most closely concerned with protecting Italian interests,
and to ask for aid for the Emperor's coming visit to
Rome to be crowned and his subsequent crusade
against the Turk. Florence fêted the embassy, but
carefully sent immediate news of its demands to France.
To the ambassadors, the reply was that it was difficult
for Florence to support the crusade, because of her
business commitments in the Levant, but she would
supply a body of horse to be used in Italy only. France
was notified, and assured that this was in no way intended to loosen relations with her. Fortunately for
Florence, an impending conflict between France and
Spain over the interpretation of the partition treaty
made Louis anxious enough to preserve his communications through Tuscany to affirm his protection.

Florence soon had cause to invoke it, as the third phase of Cesare Borgia's campaign to unite papal lands got under way. Central Italy was to Italy as a whole what Italy was to Europe: a mêlée of self-interested powers that made united opposition to an aggressor impossible. Throughout the Romagna, Umbria, and the Marches, each district, each town, had characteristics which prompted it to scorn the others, and had, moreover, internal feuds of its own. The factors causing disorder in this area were many. The ruling families themselves, splendid as some of them were—like the Baglioni in Perugia—dared not exert their authority too far for fear of revolt. A constant irritant was the presence of exiles, ever watchful for a chance of returning to their native cities; another was the readiness of factions to call in 'foreign' aid in times of stress. If a quarrel was sought, there was always a cause: the network of marriages and of various degrees of protection meant that there were ample excuses for changing sides or breaking an agreement. The chief aristocratic occupation was war, and constant raiding meant that food was often in short supply, and pestilence hard to check; men therefore chose to go out after military adventure rather than to stay in discomfort and danger at home. The ideal of chivalrous splendour involved expenses that could only be recouped by war, and as there was a lively cult of military glory even among the tax-paying bourgeoisie, there was no brake on the alternation of raid and revel.

In this region Cesare could pick his chestnuts out of the fire one at a time, demonstrating the driving power of a prince who followed ruthlessly his own strenuous course. He began operations when fine weather came in the spring. With him was Piero dei Medici, and among his captains was Vitellozzo, the brother of Florence's victim Paolo Vitelli. The first move was made against Florence's most southerly dominion, the Val di Chiana which runs down from Arezzo to Montepulciano, though Cesare himself remained in Rome and professed to know nothing of this threat to the possessions of a state protected by France; all overt action was taken by Vitellozzo, who intrigued with the anti-Florentine faction in Arezzo to such good effect that on approaching with his troops, the citizens besieged the garrison in their quarters and welcomed the Borgian army. The rest of the Val di Chiana rapidly followed suit, the inhabitants not wishing to lose their harvest, and, being asked to surrender in the name of the Medici, felt that this saved their action from being downright treachery.

When the news from Arezzo reached Florence, aid was asked from France, and the troops blockading Pisa (there were not enough for an assault) were switched to the Val di Chiana under their captain, Antonio Giacomini, a Florentine, much admired for his military skill and straightforward republican zeal by Machiavelli, who was in constant touch with him through the Ten. He held his few troops back, waiting for French reinforcements before entering the Val di Chiana, and, while they were waiting, a request came from Cesare that Florence should send him envoys to discuss the whole situation. Two men were chosen; Francesco Soderini, bishop of Volterra, and—as his colleague and assistant—Machiavelli, who had dealt with much of the correspondence concerning the crisis.

During the previous eighteen months Cesare Borgia had established himself not only as a successful military leader and an imperious statesman but as an ogre. Tales were told of wanton cruelty, of his indiscriminate lust for both sexes, his treachery; his men were said to sell women by the cartload and, although led by the son of the Pope, to stable their horses in churches. While the envoys were on their way, they heard of his latest *coup*. He had begged the assistance of Duke Guidobaldo of Urbino in an attack on Camerino. The Duke, as a feudatory of the Pope and a friend of Cesare's had agreed, but when his troops and artillery were on the way Cesare dashed behind him and occupied his city so that, as the envoys reported, 'his death was heard of before he was known to be ill'.

So it was at Urbino that Cesare received them, and he received them with high confidence, demanding that they stop intriguing against him with the common ally, France, and straightway change their government into a form which he personally could trust. As for Arezzo—that affair, he claimed, had been undertaken with French approval.

The Florentines were not there to negotiate but to listen and report, and they left two days later. Their final dispatch, written in the small hours after a second interview, ended with a portrait: 'This lord is very proud and fine, and as a soldier is so enterprising that nothing is so great that it does not seem small to him, and for the sake of glory and of acquiring lands he does not rest, and acknowledges no fatigue or danger. He arrives at one place before he is known to have left the other; he endears himself to his soldiers; he has got hold of the best men in Italy, and these factors, to-

gether with continual good fortune, make him victorious and dangerous.' The dispatch was signed by
Soderini, but here we have Machiavelli's first written
judgment on the man whose activity had been making
the pens fly in the secretariats of the Second Chancery
and the Ten.

Florence did nothing to follow up this embassy.
French aid arrived and the Val di Chiana was speedily
reduced. The problem was then how to treat the rebels,
for without the active co-operation of the inhabitants
Vitellozzo would have been helpless. It was treated
by Machiavelli himself in a short discourse, *On the
Method of Dealing with the Rebels of the Val di
Chiana*. This was something new for him. It was not a
conventional departmental report, like the Pisan one
or a report he had drawn up in the previous year on
the state of affairs in Pistoia, and it was written retro-
spectively between June 1st and August 18th, 1503.

His opening words were, 'Lucius Furius Cammillus,
after defeating the rebellious peoples of Latium . . .',
and Machiavelli proceeded to devote nearly half his
space to the episode described by Livy when the Senate
decided how it was to treat the conquered rebels. They
determined to win over the more loyal cities by
kindness, but utterly ruin the rest, for the Romans,
Machiavelli observed, 'thought any middle way to be
dangerous'. He then justifies his use of this analogy. 'I
have heard that history is the teacher of our actions,
and especially of our rulers; the world has always been
inhabited by men with the same passions as our own,
and there have always been rulers and ruled, and good
subjects and bad subjects, and those who rebel and are
punished.' Florence had been lenient towards the coun-

try people of the Val di Chiana, and this Machiavelli approved, but he did not approve of the hesitant treatment of Arezzo itself. 'If it is true that history is the teacher of our actions it would be good for those who have to determine the fate of the Val di Chiana to follow their example and imitate those who were masters of the world, especially in a case where they show exactly what you should do.' With part, but only part, of its citizens fined and exiled and with the walls left standing, Arezzo would still be ready to break into fresh rebellion, a matter of no slight importance, with Cesare Borgia at hand, seeking to form a strong state by getting Tuscany itself into his power. 'And I remember hearing it said to Cardinal Soderini that among the other titles of greatness that should be given to the Duke and the Pope was this : they were masterly judges of an opportunity, and could turn it to the best advantage.'

Cesare had been unreasonable in his demand that Florence should readmit the Medici, but his complaints that Florence could not be trusted were, like the French complaints to the same effect, largely justified. Government in Florence was on the point of breaking down. At the time of the Val di Chiana affair, Guicciardini noted in his *History of Florence*, 'the city was in such disorder and peril that things had hardly been so bad since the king of France came to Florence'. Then, the city had been saved from anarchy by Savonarola's republican constitution. Now this in its turn was failing : a victim to party strife and inefficiency. There was chronic conflict between rich and poor. At each crisis—Pisa in 1500, Cesare Borgia in Tuscany in 1501, and now Arezzo—there was class recrimination. The less wealthy bourgeois suspected the *grandi* of governing for their own advantage alone, imposing taxes ostensibly for war but actually for their own profit—it was even thought that the news from Arezzo was exaggerated so that they would have an excuse to cancel operations against Pisa, and this in spite of the choice of Giacomini, which was a deliberate attempt to placate popular opposition. The *grandi* themselves were kept divided by the constant possibility of the return of the Medici, who appeared among the lances of every Florentine enemy. And while the ordinary citizen suspected and resented the influence of the *grandi* on the various bodies that comprised the government, many of the *grandi* themselves were alienated by the system of rotation that gave the government a popular tone, and it was certainly true that rotation brought many second-rate men into office without leaving them there long enough to learn the job or acquire a sense of responsibility.

The defects of the constitution were of a sort that became most apparent in a time of crisis. Rotation—and the gonfalonier of justice, the nominal head of the government, was himself only in office for two months, and could not be re-elected for three years—meant that there was no permanent authority to see that decisions once taken were carried through. There were elaborate safety devices to prevent any individuals or single families from acquiring too much power, and this tended to rob the government of the weight and experience it needed. Whirled with such rapidity through their period of office, many men were more concerned with lining their pockets than benefiting the state, and the amount of peculation was a serious social abrasive. The public withheld tax payments as a result, and the government had to rely increasingly on forced loans from the rich, a process which further exasperated class antagonisms and made many responsible men refuse state employment—so that the state had to lean more heavily than ever on inexperienced men.

It was generally agreed that reform was necessary, but in what shape? Could increased efficiency be won without the loss of liberty? No party was prepared to touch the Great Council which, more than any other body, represented the republican principle of wide consent. The great hall in which it met, for which Leonardo and Michelangelo had been commissioned to paint frescoes, was looked on as the shrine of the constitution; it was a gesture charged with significance when the Medici later divided it up to house their soldiery. An aristocratic proposal to set up a permanent senate, on similar lines to that of Venice, was rejected as potentially oligarchic, but another Venetian parallel was taken up; Florence would have a doge in the shape of a permanent gonfalonier. It was felt that while this avoided the central issue of inefficiency, it would reassure foreign powers that when Florence accepted a policy she would abide by it. There were three main candidates for the new office, and it went to the most moderate and least committed of them, Piero Soderini, brother of Machiavelli's recent colleague, the bishop of Volterra. The appointment did give a measure of strength to Florence, though Soderini proved over-hesitant and cautious, and it was of considerable moment to Machiavelli's career. Soderini was a man with no party: the fact that he had no children and few relatives had been thought a

point in his favour; he relied on the secretariat, and
very soon he came to rely especially on Machiavelli.
For Machiavelli this was a mixed blessing. It enhanced
his prestige and gave him some voice in affairs, but it
marked him as a Soderini man, and his fortunes were
henceforward bound up with those of the gonfalonier.

The influence of the change on outside opinion was
soon to be tested. Cesare Borgia's successes—one small
state after another falling into his hands—had aroused
the jealousy of his captains. On October 9th they met
at Magione, near the east shore of Lake Trasimene
and discussed what measures they could use against
him. The first action taken by the Confederacy of
Magione, as the group came to be called, was the
capture of Urbino. Both sides asked Florence for help,
Cesare requesting an embassy to discuss the situation
especially in the light of his Florentine military contract of 1501. He suggested that Florence could best
help him by making demonstrations in the north-west
Romagna to draw off the confederates and dismay
them. The Florentines were unwilling to commit
themselves, and adopted the usual expedient of sending not an ambassador but a mandatory—Machiavelli
—to play for time, to assure Cesare of Florence's
friendship without doing anything in particular to
prove it.

The commission was dated October 5th. By the 7th
Machiavelli was already with the Duke at Imola. In
contrast with the briefness of his last meeting, he was to
be with Cesare for over three months, returning to
Florence on February 23rd, 1503. In one of his earliest
dispatches he mentioned the new constitution in terms
that must have given great pleasure in the Palazzo

della Signoria, for referring to Cesare's suggestion that he should be made commander of the Florentine forces, he added that 'he wants to wait, before the matter goes any further, until the next gonfalonier has been installed in his palace; for this new order of things has raised the credit of Florence to a degree that no one could have believed'.

Machiavelli's task, however, was not to negotiate with Cesare Borgia, save to ensure safe conduct for Florentine merchants across his domains, but to analyse the state of affairs between the Duke and the confederates and define in which direction the wind seemed to be blowing; his city's enhanced reputation could do nothing to help him here. Information was hard to come by. Reports of the numbers and intentions of both sides were conflicting, he was in touch only with the Borgian point of view, and this could be misleading, for Cesare was secretive and devious, and even when one of his confidants volunteered information Machiavelli found it hard to decide if it were not merely an attempt to mislead him. He was careful to give the status and character of his informants, so that the Ten could judge what weight to give their opinions, and he repeatedly warned them that he was too near to one particular interest to give a clear judgment on the whole situation.

He did, nevertheless, attempt from time to time a general statement. On October 27th, for instance, he wrote from Imola a dispatch in which he tried to forecast in what way the present *impasse* between the duke and the rebels might be resolved.

'If we examine the characters of both one and the other party, we shall find in the Duke a daring and fortunate man, full of hope, favoured by a pope and a king, and who finds himself assailed by others not only in a state which he wishes to acquire [Bologna], but also in one which he has acquired already [Urbino]. The other party will be seen to fear for their own states, and to have been afraid of the Duke before they provoked him. Having done so now, their fears are increased, and it is impossible to see how the latter can pardon the offence, or how the former can cease to fear him, and, consequently, how either the one can yield in his attempt against Bologna, or the others in theirs upon the duchy of Urbino.

'It is argued that an amicable agreement between them would be possible only if they could unite their joint forces against some third party, in which case neither the Duke nor the confederates need reduce their forces, and both would rather gain in fact and in renown. However, if such an arrangement could be brought about, there would be no other power for them to turn against except Florence or Venice. An attack on Florence is thought to be the easier of the two, so far as Florence itself is concerned, but more difficult on account of the king of France; while an attempt on Venice would be easier so far as the king of France is concerned but more difficult as regards Venice itself. The latter would be most agreeable to the duke, and the former to the confederates. Still, it is not believed that either, though spoken of as possible, will actually be undertaken.

'Thus I can find no one who can definitely suggest a basis for agreement between them. But those who do form some definite idea on the subject believe that the duke will succeed in causing a split amongst the confederates and having thus broken up their alliance he will have nothing more to fear from them, and can then carry on with his own projects. . . . The league, however, is so recent, that it is difficult to believe in its being broken up.'

As it turned out, the parties were ostensibly reconciled at the end of the month. Machiavelli warned his government not to take this at its face value. On November 3rd he reported rumours which suggested that the Duke was meditating revenge on his faithless captains, and though relations between them continued peaceable, the last recalcitrant rebel signing a treaty with Cesare on December 2nd, he still thought revenge was intended. From Cesena on December 14th he pointed out that Cesare had not dismissed the French troops he had called for when the crisis was at its height, 'and although the treaties of peace would seem to oppose this conclusion, yet the example of the past would make these treaties of less consequence.' He could not believe that Cesare was one of the few men who could forget injuries done to them in the past.

While he was away, Machiavelli received frequent letters from his chancery colleagues, Buonaccorsi alone writing once or twice a week with news about the department and about Marietta. It was clear that his dispatches were being well received. Buonaccorsi wrote one letter, on October 28th, in which he blamed Machiavelli for not writing enough, being too definite in his opinions, and for giving views at the expense of news (news, as Machiavelli explained, was exactly what he was short of), but on other occasions Buonaccorsi says that he praised Machiavelli's dispatches to Soderini himself. From another colleague, Niccolò

Valori, came uniformly glowing reports. 'All acknow-
ledge,' he wrote on October 11th, 'what I have specially noted in you, a clear, sensible and straightforward
mode of narration, on which one can really rely.' On
the 23rd he praised Machiavelli's dispatches again,
and declared that if everyone had Machiavelli's ability
fewer mistakes would be made, and on the 31st he
returned to the same theme, singling out Machiavelli's
vigorous style and good judgment for special congratu-
lation. Machiavelli was not only praised for the official
parts of his letters. Another colleague, Bartolomeo
Ruffini, wrote on October 23rd to describe how
Machiavelli on one occasion had caused all his readers
to laugh themselves into stitches.

Frustrating as the mission was from the point of view
of information and forecast, Machiavelli was clearly
intrigued by watching Cesare at close quarters. 'The
Duke,' he wrote on November 8th, 'cannot be considered like other petty princes . . . but must be regarded
as a new power in Italy.' And clearly the Duke had
some relish for Machiavelli's company, calling him to
long audiences in which no definite political purpose
was apparent. Machiavelli's account of one of these
conversations gives its mood well, its casual, ruthless
assumption of change and conquest. Cesare had been
speaking of the haughty but canny Venetians, 'and of
the honours they had shown to an agent of his whom
he had sent to buy some guns. . . . He then spoke of the
affair of Pisa . . . and he expressed the opinion that its
capture would be the most glorious achievement that
any captain could accomplish. From that the Duke
suddenly turned the conversation upon Lucca, saying
that it was a rich city, and a fine morsel for a gour-

mand; and so we passed a considerable time in similar conversation.' Nor was the realism all on one side. Soon after his arrival at Imola, Machiavelli passed on the Duke's request that Florentine troops should make a show of strength on his behalf and added, 'You could raise yourself still more in the Duke's estimation by representing the number double what they really are; for the Duke will not be able to get reliable information.' To one of Cesare's chief ministers he maintained that 'alliances between princes are ensured only by arms, for the power of arms alone enforces their observance', and he elaborated this theme to the Duke himself, as he reported on November 20th, declaring that 'mere general friendships impose no obligations, and are readily changed in the course of time, that good and ill fortune do not remain always on the same side, that every day alliances are contracted where there is no question of permanence.' And in the same letter he shows that he is voicing the general attitude. 'Everyone here is suspicious of this lord's preparations for war in the middle of peace negotiations, especially when it is considered how much good faith one can expect in these days.' Machiavelli was not flattered by the Duke's attentions into taking him at his word.

As in France, the fascination of watching great political figures in action did not compensate for a prolonged absence from Florence. He wrote asking to be recalled as early as October 23rd, and repeated the request more urgently from Cesena on December 14th. His plea was not answered, and his friends reported that Soderini wished him to stay on. It was after this attempt to get away, in fact, that there occurred events so sensational that he dwelt on them in his later writings. Cesare Borgia's chief agent in the pacification and administration of the Romagna was Ramiro Lorqua. On December 26th Machiavelli wrote: 'This morning Messer Ramiro has been found cut in two pieces on the piazza [at Cesena] where he still lies, and all the people have been able to see him; the reason for his death is not well known, excepting that such was the pleasure of the prince, who shows us that he can make and unmake men according to their deserts.' There was at least one other purpose: Ramiro was an enemy of Paolo Orsini, one of the ex-confederates, whom Cesare was devotedly lulling to their destruction.

He arranged to meet them—Orsini, together with the duke of Gravina (also a member of the Orsini family), Oliverotto da Fermo, and Vitellozzo Vitelli— at Senigallia, which they had captured at the end of December, ostensibly to celebrate the success of their joint enterprise. Cesare entered on December 31st, met the ex-rebel captains and took them to his quarters. In the course of their conference he made an excuse to leave the room, whereupon his men swarmed in and took them prisoners while their troops were attacked and disarmed outside in the town. Machiavelli wrote while the uproar was still going on. 'I do not know if I can send this letter, having no one to carry it. It is my opinion that they [the prisoners] will not be alive tomorrow.' In part he was right; Vitellozzo and Oliverotto were strangled that night.[1] Machiavelli's letter was written just before sunset. Two hours later, he was sent for by the Duke 'who, with the brightest face in the world, expressed his satisfaction at this triumph.' And

---

[1] The Duke of Gravina and Paolo Orsini were killed later, on January 18th.

Cesare added—'this is what I wanted to tell the bishop [Soderini] about back in Urbino, but I never trust a secret.'

The Duke's action was widely praised, the historian Nardi going so far as to write of him as the instrument of divine justice. Chivalric morality was still alive to this extent: if a man betrayed his lord, any fate was good enough for him. An affair of this sort was different from the betrayal of one state by another; it was still a matter for some scruples, it concerned not alliance but allegiance, where the offender had no rights. For Machiavelli the episode had a more complex appeal. For two months he had lived half expecting such a *dénouement*, though he can hardly have expected to find himself an eyewitness of anything quite so drastic. His *Description of the Manner in which Duke Valentino put Vitellozzo Vitelli, Oliverotto da Fermo, Paolo and the Duke of Gravina Orsini to Death*, written after his return to Florence, shows how the combination of violence and cunning appealed to the writer, the dramatist, in him. This literary version of the Senigallia episode differs in several respects from the version given in his dispatches; there are purely literary touches like the dying remarks of Oliverotto and Vitellozzo, and situations are altered to make Cesare seem in full control of every move (whereas in reality the suspicious captains had only just been persuaded to join him) and to emphasize the precision and neatness of his planning. But the episode appealed, too, as an allegory of necessary political ruthlessness on any scale. Finally it is perhaps not ingenuous to include a certain proprietary

interest in a scene where he himself had played a part,
even if only that of a walker-on.

Senigallia certainly increased his admiration for
Cesare. 'People here,' he wrote on January 8th, 'won-
der that you have not written, or in some way sent your
congratulations to the Duke.' It was Cesare's view that
Florence was greatly in his debt for ridding her of so
many potential enemies—especially Vitellozzo, always
seeking revenge for his brother's death, and Machiavelli agreed. But in spite of having anticipated Senigallia, he remained cautious about foretelling the political
future. When Cesare next took Perugia and then
turned towards Siena, with the intention of turning out
its ruler Pandolfo Petrucci, Machiavelli was as judicial
as ever. 'On the one hand there is the Duke, with his
unheard of good fortune, with a courage and confidence almost superhuman, and believing himself
capable of accomplishing whatever he undertakes; and
on the other there is a man at the head of a state of
high reputation which he governs with great sagacity,
and without an enemy either foreign or domestic,
having either conciliated or put them to death, and
having plenty of good troops. . . . There is nothing else
to be done but to wait and see the end.' Petrucci fled,
in fact, after the Sienese countryside had been terror-
ized by the Duke's men, but before this happened
Florence had sent a full ambassador to relieve Machiavelli, who returned to Florence on January 23rd.

With spring, the Florentines wished to take up the
Pisan campaign, but were faced by a crucial difficulty
—how to raise the money. There were long and bitter
discussions about the fairest form of tax, the *grandi*
wanting something that would weigh equally on all,

the poorer citizens wanting the main charge to fall on
the *grandi*. In the Palazzo della Signoria there was
probably much discussion over the line Soderini should
follow, and Machiavelli's contribution took the form of
an imaginary speech [1] which the gonfalonier might
have delivered in the Great Council. Soderini is known
to have spoken impressively on this theme, but he is
hardly likely to have used Machiavelli's draft, for
Machiavelli does not face the problem of what sort of
tax is to be used, he simply sermonizes on the theme
that money *must* be found. He was not interested in
finance, but in the military use of cash, and sprang
straight into general advice based on his experience
both of the dangers that faced Florence and the poor
esteem in which she was held by other powers.

The life gonfaloniership has helped, he begins, but
for real security you must raise money, as states today
are only respected if they have armies. It is folly to
think that alliances will protect you, 'for whereas laws,
agreements and contracts bind private individuals to
keep faith, arms alone count with princes.' You must
make yourself respected, otherwise you have no bargaining power with your chief connection, France.
Remembering that the crises caused by Cesare Borgia's
demands in 1501 and the revolt of Arezzo were caused
by Florence's having dismissed most of her hired
troops, he points out 'that one cannot always use
another's sword, and therefore it is well to keep your
own in readiness and girded on, even when the enemy
is far off'. And he concluded with an urgent plea for
action : 'I tell you that Fortune can not help those who
will not help themselves, nor would—or could—heaven

[1] *Parole sopra la provvisione del danaio.*

itself sustain a thing that is determined to fall.' If Florence was to count for something in the modern world, if she was to give the lie to France's contemptuous 'Mr. Nothing', she must be strong. Strength was measured in soldiers and guns, therefore money must be raised.

The impatient tone of this harangue, the first important utterance in the canon of his political writings, owes much to his diplomatic experience. Having seen Florence from the outside, he was more concerned for the effect she made on other powers than on the internal processes that would produce that effect; he was interested in foreign affairs more than in domestic politics. As a civil servant he knew intimately, from tedious and at times humiliating personal experience, the hesitations and changes of front of his own government. Doubtless the chanceries of Louis XII and Cesare Borgia reflected some degree of the same inefficiency, but he saw only the effects of their statecraft, incisive and resolute. His own energetic temperament suggested that resolution was better than hesitancy; his observation of foreign states confirmed it.

Florence's position became more hazardous as Cesare's fortunes continued to prosper. He lost Siena, indeed. France and Florence restored Pandolfo in March and Machiavelli went to confer with him at the end of April. But the Borgias, anxious now for a free hand in central Italy, were encouraged not only by fresh, if small successes there, but by continued French reverses in the south, culminating in a striking victory for the Spaniards at Cerignola, a battle which established the fame of Gonsalvo of Cordova as one of the greatest generals of his day. Cesare was only stopped in a fresh attempt on Siena, Pisa, and Florence itself by the entry into Italy of a new French expedition aimed at Naples. It was at this juncture that his father, Alexander VI, was taken ill and died in Rome on August 18th, at a time when Cesare was ill himself.

The death of the pope who was believed to have bribed his way to office, committed incest with his daughter, and had some of his closest ecclesiastical associates murdered for the sake of their riches, and was known to have done more than any other pope in living memory to increase the temporal authority of the papacy in Italy, was an occasion of great significance for every Italian state, and for none more than for Florence. Without the promise of further papal support, Cesare's states began to disintegrate; one by one the old owners returned: the Baglioni to Perugia, the Montefeltro to Urbino; Pesaro and Rimini recalled their former lords, the Florentines took back Piombino, the Venetians took over Faenza. But with Cesare still alive and some of his Romagna lands still faithful to him, these actions were tentative; the future was uncertain.

It became more uncertain than ever when Pius III, elected as a stop-gap, died even sooner than expected, on October 18th. The next choice would certainly be a more lasting one. Cesare was well again and at Rome. Fearful both of him and of Venetian readiness to take advantage of any confusion in the Romagna, Florence was unable to wait until the new election had been made. Machiavelli was sent to Rome as an observer on October 23rd.

He arrived four days later to find that one candidate, Giuliano della Rovere, cardinal of S. Pietro in

Vincola, was much the strongest; he was elected Pope Julius II on November 1st. The new Pope, Machiavelli wrote, 'will have enough to do to fulfil all the promises he has made [to buy votes in the conclave], for many of them are contradictory'. In fact, the policies of Julius II, who was to become a figure even more respected and feared than Alexander had been, were at first exploratory. He was short of money, and played for time until he was sure of the strength of his own position. For this reason, and because matters between France and Spain were at pause, their armies eyeing one another across the river Garigliano, some ninety miles to the south, Machiavelli found most interest in the declining fortunes of Cesare Borgia, and the combination of that interest with the congenial company he met in Rome—among others his former chief at Urbino, bishop Soderini, now a cardinal, was there—made him for the first time reluctant to bring a mission to an end and return home. And this in spite of the birth of a son soon after his departure. The boy was baptized on November 9th, with two chancery colleagues, Marcello Virgilio Adriani and Buonaccorsi, as godfathers, and Marietta wrote on the 24th to say how much she was missing him and how frightened she was at news of plague in Rome. 'The baby is well, and is like you. He is as white as snow, but he has what looks like black velvet on his head, and he is as hairy as you are, and since he is like you I find him handsome. He looks as if he had already been in the world for a year, and he opened his eyes before he was hardly born, and filled the whole house with noise.'

It was Machiavelli's first sight of Rome, but though a student of Livy, he must not be imagined as bringing

to it the emotions of the later Grand Tourist. He was
less interested in precipitating himself back into the
Roman past than in applying its lessons to the present.
There is no evidence that he had any of the instincts
of the archaeologist or the student of literary associations. But Rome was the centre of Italian politics, the
main clearing-house for international news, and for
rumours and alarms it provided the most nourishing
air in Europe. For Machiavelli its appeal was rather
that of an experimental laboratory than a museum.

He had written of Cesare Borgia on the eve of the
papal election : 'It is generally thought that whoever
may be elected Pope will be under great obligation to
the Duke [because of his influence on the Spanish
cardinals], who lives in the hope of being supported by the new Pope.' And at first Julius flattered
Cesare with promises of support. 'The Duke allows
himself,' wrote Machiavelli on November 4th, 'to be
carried away by his sanguine confidence, believing that
the word of others is more to be relied on than his
own.' This confidence was by now vulnerable, however. Machiavelli went to see him after the news of
Venice's attack on Faenza had reached Rome. The
duke wildly abused Florence for having let this happen. 'I lacked neither matter nor words to answer him',
Machiavelli reported on November 6th, 'and yet I
thought it best to soothe him, and managed as adroitly
as I could to break off the interview which seemed to
me to have lasted a thousand years.'

In spite of the obvious cooling of Machiavelli's admiration for the Duke, it was felt in Florence that his
study of the situation in the Romagna could be
achieved without making so close a personal study of

Cesare. Buonaccorsi warned him on November 15th
that it was even being rumoured that Machiavelli was
hoping for some patronage from him. But the fascination was strong, and Machiavelli took no notice. The
roles were changing. The Duke was now the uncertain
one, Machiavelli the man who was sure of himself.
Commenting on Cesare's lack of grip, Machiavelli
noted that 'this may be the result of his natural character, or because the blows of fortune, which he is not
accustomed to bear, have stunned and confounded
him'. From mere observer, Machiavelli became a
manipulator of the Duke's fortunes. Cesare had asked
for a safe conduct for his troops to march north across
Tuscany. Florence refused, but Machiavelli softened
the blow by suggesting that an arrangement might still
be reached. 'Your lordships will observe that my
answers to the Duke were only intended to give some
little encouragement to his hopes, so that he might
have no excuse for remaining here any longer, and so
that the Pope, in his desire to get rid of him, might not
oblige you to give the Duke the safe conduct he wants.'

On the 26th it was rumoured that the Duke, who
had left Rome and was waiting for shipping at Ostia,
had been taken prisoner on the Pope's orders. Machiavelli's comment was brief. 'Since the Duke is taken,
whether dead or alive, we can now act regardless of
him.' And he goes on with a reference to his post-
election dispatch. 'We now see how honourably this
Pope begins to pay his debts, and how he wipes them out
as with a sponge.' Cesare was not dead but a prisoner,
and trying to bargain with Julius over the surrender of
his Romagna fortresses. But he was bargaining from a
weak position against a strengthening one. 'And thus

the Duke,' wrote Machiavelli on December 3rd, 'is little by little slipping into his grave.' Though he wrote other dispatches from Rome, this was his last reference to Cesare Borgia.

He left for Florence on December 18th, and hard on his heels came news of a battle on the Garigliano in which the French had been resoundingly defeated. Florence, already perturbed by Venetian pretensions on her Romagna frontier and short, as usual, of money and troops, was aghast at this unexpected news, speedily followed as it was by rumours that Gonsalvo was preparing to march north on Milan, relieving Pisa on the way. There was already a Florentine ambassador in France, Niccolò Valori, but the new hazard was too grave for communication by dispatch; an envoy was needed, and Machiavelli was chosen.

This role was hardly more than that of a special courier, but it is an interesting sign of his growing repute that whereas he had been criticized for including speculation in his dispatches from the headquarters of Cesare Borgia, his instructions on this mission to France specifically asked for his 'conjecture and opinion'. Valori, the resident ambassador, was an old friend and made much of him, mentioning him from time to time in his dispatches. He described the tact he showed with the King's secretary Robertet, and how he put Florence's plight to d'Amboise 'with that animation which the subject demanded', soothing the irascible cardinal at one point 'with his wonted sagacity and adroitness'. It was clear that France thought Florence was showing a needless agitation. The great powers had stretched themselves as far as their resources could easily allow; a pause for recuperation was needed. In fact, a three years' truce between France and Spain was signed at Lyons on February 11th which extended its protection to Florence as an ally of France. This meant that for three years Florence was to be able to concentrate on Italian affairs, notably the Pisan war. Valori asked d'Amboise what Florence should do about Pisa in the light of the truce, and the cardinal's reply showed that her client-status had not improved since Machiavelli's last French mission. 'His Eminence let fall the following words, which seemed to me worth noting : "Keep yourselves well prepared and provided, and leave us to think and do the rest."'

CHAPTER FOUR

Pisa and the Militia: 1504–1506

———————

THE truce meant that Machiavelli could return. The government was busy with Pisan plans, both diplomatic and military. An embassy was sent in March to congratulate Gonsalvo on his successes in Naples and to try to discover his future intentions. Because it was rumoured that Iacopo d'Appiano of Piombino was thinking of aiding Pisa, Machiavelli was sent on April 2nd to persuade him to aid Florence instead. In May Giampaolo Baglioni and other captains were engaged. Giacomini was made commissary-general. Galleys were hired to blockade Pisa by sea. On land the harvest was destroyed. But the galleys were sunk in a storm, and supplies were somehow smuggled in from Genoa, Lucca, and Siena.

When the sea blockade failed, an attempt was made to cut off this supply route from the other end, by diverting the Arno altogether and depriving Pisa of her sea road. This plan was considered by many as extravagant folly, and Soderini was defeated when he first proposed it. He managed to push the scheme through, however, and for Machiavelli the months of August and September were devoted to the service of this sensational failure. The scheme involved turning the Arno from its course near Cascina, and running its waters into dykes which would discharge into the sea north of Livorno, thus leaving Pisa high and dry. It was estimated, optimistically, that to dam the Arno and dig the dykes it would take two thousand pioneers three weeks. No one but Soderini and Machiavelli seemed convinced by these figures or that the plan would work. Bentivoglio produced a far more gloomy estimate of the labour force required, and Giacomini, after setting the recruitment of pioneers in motion, pleaded sick and asked to be relieved. It was prophesied that the gradient between Cascina and Livorno would prove too slight to carry the water away, but in spite of this the work proceeded under the direction of canal experts from Lombardy—the scene of Italy's most ambitious water engineering to this date.

Machiavelli was tireless in supporting them, writing great numbers of letters to the mayors of local communes about labourers and their equipment, but the work still went much more slowly than had been planned. The gradient did turn out to be too shallow, and, even more serious, the narrowing gap of the dam forced the water to run more swiftly, thus scouring the river bed down below the level of entry into the dykes. The rainy season found operations still going forward, but the labourers began to desert *en masse*, and work had to be called off, whereupon the Pisans lost no time in filling up the deserted ditches.

Machiavelli used the leisure brought him by the cessation of hostilities to write his first ambitious literary work, *The First Decade*, a verse chronicle in *terza rima* devoted to the events of the ten years from Charles VIII's invasion. In his dedication to Alamanno Salviati, who had been a member of the Signoria during the Arezzo crisis, which is dated November 9th,

he says that the poem is the result of a fortnight's work.
Not surprisingly, its five hundred and fifty lines are
bold rather than beautiful, but among the somewhat
jogging lines are a few phrases of real imaginative
power, and the narrative is fast and coherent. With
its cryptic and recondite allusions to contemporary
events and personalities, it was written for immediate
consumption for an audience drawn more from men
of affairs than from the people. This is acknowledged
in Agostino Vespucci's preface to a printed edition
which he produced for Machiavelli in 1506. Referring
to the poem and to a larger historical work on which
Machiavelli was engaged, he said the poem was for
contemporaries, the other work for posterity, 'who
would be puzzled by the compression' of *The First
Decade*.

Machiavelli's theme is the woes of an Italy whose
divisions left a way open for the barbarians. Politically,
it is a cautious document, as indeed it had to be if it
were to be read in influential circles. He refers to the
Medici, but not in a constitutional context; one aspect
of his ten-year theme, he makes it clear, is the disinte-
gration of territories won for Florence by the Medici.
While the poem is dedicated to the influential and con-
servative Salviati, to whom there are also flattering
references in the text, Machiavelli refers warmly to
Piero Soderini, the *soda petra* (solid stone) on which
Florentine unity has been based since the creation of
the life gonfaloniership. But while deferential to Florentine personalities, he is sometimes scathing in his
references to the city as a whole—to her helpless reliance on the French in 1495, for instance, when 'You
waited with your beak open for someone who would

bring you manna in the desert'; that is, return Pisa and
the northern fortresses. 'That great Savonarola' is
lashed for the party strife he caused, and Machiavelli
shows the cruder side of his tongue when he refers to
the friar's 'divine light quenched with a more powerful
flame'. Cesare Borgia is spoken of with admiration for
his conquests, and for the way in which he 'gently
whistled' the Magione confederates into his trap at
Senigallia, but he is scorned in defeat and mocked for
his trust in Julius II, in whom 'he expected to find the
pity he himself had never felt'. The betrayal by Gonsalvo was what 'a rebel to Christ' deserved; so ended
the career of one 'who once caused you to tremble
and Rome weep'.

The poem ends with a foreboding epilogue. For ten
years the world has been stained with blood. The
present calm is illusory; the seeds of further discord
remain. He lists them: the Pope, anxious to recover
the Church's lands; France, smarting from the Spanish
defeat; Spain, intriguing to preserve her conquests;
Venice, hovering between peace and war, timorous yet
voracious; Florence herself, intent on the recovery of
Pisa. For these reasons, he concludes, 'My whole mind
is on fire now with hope, now with fear, so that little
by little it is consumed; I would dearly like to know
where our vessel, so heavily burdened, is likely to be
driven by these winds.' Soderini is at the helm; that is
something. 'But', the poem ends, 'the road would be
easy and short if you were to reopen Mars's temple.' If
Florence were armed, in fact, there would be no need
to wait for others to bring her manna in the desert.

The only contemporary opinion of the poem that is
known is that of Ercole Bentivoglio, who was given

a copy of Vespucci's printed edition. The captain-general of the Florentine forces praised the deftness with which the long and complicated story had been compressed by Machiavelli, and urged him to continue the work, though it was sad business remembering such tragic events. But a record of them was useful to show posterity that Italy was not simply the victim of her own indifference to honour and liberty; without this evidence they would never be able to appreciate the former prosperity of Italy or how she had come so soon to fall so far. He ended his letter to Machiavelli by saying that things still looked black, 'unless he who saved the Israelites from the hands of Pharaoh should open an unexpected way of safety across this varying sea, as he did for them'. The warrior had missed the civilian's point; Machiavelli was invoking not Jehovah but the god of war.

The greater storm clouds still held off, and 1505 was again a Pisan year. The campaigning season started badly, with the Florentines defeated by a Pisan army at Ponte a Cappellese in March, and for a while the familiar roles were reversed, with Pisa preventing much-needed corn supplies from Livorno from reaching Florence. The situation was all the more serious because of the existence of a large freelance condottiere band under Bartolomeo d'Alviano—till recently a colleague of Gonsalvo—who was leagued with a number of families who had grudges against the Florentines, including the Vitelli. Even Giampaolo Baglioni, still in Florentine pay, was suspected of being of this faction, which was believed to be aiming at the relief of Pisa, but when challenged by Florence he refused to commit himself one way or the other.

In April Machiavelli was sent to Perugia to see how matters stood. Giampaolo attempted to plead that pressure from domestic enemies prevented him from honouring his engagement with Florence, whereupon Machiavelli preached the general a fine sermon on the theme of a Gentleman's Word. Everyone knew he had accepted the money, Machiavelli pointed out, and 'would therefore never excuse him, but would charge him with ingratitude and bad faith, and would regard him as a stumbling horse which nobody would ride for fear of getting his neck broken; that matters of this kind were not to be judged by learned doctors but by gentlemen; and that whoever attached any value to wearing armour, and desired to win honour by his arms, could lose nothing that was prized so much as a reputation for good faith'. And more in the same vein. Machiavelli continues this dispatch of April 11th. 'And thus I pricked him right and left, speaking to him as a friend, and as though this were merely coming from me; but although I noticed several times that he changed countenance, yet he gave no indication that could make me hope he would change his determination.' Machiavelli came away with nothing more definite than a conviction that there was a plot in the air and Giampaolo was not to be trusted.

Florence then tried to secure the services of the Marquis of Mantua as captain-general, and sent Machiavelli to Mantua in May to hasten the negotiations, but the Marquis haggled so long that the deal fell through. Florence was becoming more and more perturbed, Spanish soldiers were rumoured to be filtering north into Piombino, and Pandolfo Petrucci was behaving very oddly; he was a confessed enemy of the

Florentines (in spite of his recent restoration with their help), but he was, nevertheless, offering to join them against Pisa. Machiavelli was sent to Siena to investigate this phenomenon in July, being given a flatteringly loose commission. 'You will treat the subject in all its bearings, for which purpose you will have to take counsel of yourself, and govern your conduct with your habitual prudence.'

In Petrucci Machiavelli found another stone-waller. On July 21st he reported to the Ten that he had pointed out how many contradictory things Petrucci had said during the past few days. Petrucci had replied by putting a leaf into Machiavelli's own book. 'I begged his Magnificence,' Machiavelli wrote, 'to explain all these contradictions to me.' Petrucci replied, 'I will answer you as king Frederick answered a similar question asked by one of my envoys; namely, that to avoid falling into error we must shape our course according to events from day to day, and must judge of things from one hour to another, for time and circumstances are more powerful than human intelligence.' Machiavelli returned to Florence no wiser than he went, save, perhaps, in worldly wisdom.

With the threat from Alviano still impending, Florence was forced to get troops where she could and put them under the command of Giacomini. On August 17th they intercepted Alviano's army as it moved up the coast road north of Piombino and defeated it at San Vincenzo. This result gave Soderini so much confidence that he forced through a resolution to proceed to a general assault against Pisa. This motion was strongly opposed by a *pratica* of the Ten but he went nevertheless to the Great Council, whose members had less to lose by failure, and won their consent. The attack was mounted in spite of open threats from Gonsalvo, who was at Piombino, to intervene on the Pisans' behalf. The army besieged Pisa and began to bombard the walls, and Machiavelli was employed both there and back in Florence with his old task of recruitment and supply. A breach was at length made, but the troops, checked once by the Pisans, refused to attack again. Gonsalvo had sent reinforcements, and the army had not the heart to mount a second assault. The camp was accordingly broken up.

The result of this year of failures was to increase Florentine disillusion with condottiere troops, leaders and men alike. Soderini, smarting with defeat, looked with increasing favour on Machiavelli's idea that Florence should reopen the temple of Mars by raising a standing army from her own subjects. On the other hand, he had learned caution; the canal scheme and the recent attack on Pisa had been undertaken in the teeth of *grandi* opposition and cost him much of his popularity. He had to contend with those who maintained that at least some of the trouble with mercenaries was to be found less in themselves than in the way they were handled by the government. He had therefore to be careful in dealing with the militia project, and to insist on a trial before lending his open consent.

The disadvantages of condottiere troops were obvious. As no one captain had enough troops of his own, bands that were frequently riddled with feuds had to fight together. There was a tendency for commanders to be overcautious about risking the lives of their own men. There was constant friction between captains and their civilian helper-watchdogs. Again, it sometimes happened that there were simply none available. In 1501, for instance, Cesare Borgia had monopolized all the best condottiere troops, and in 1502, Florence had again sought vainly for aid; the Vitelli and Orsini were still with Cesare Borgia, the marquis of Mantua had offended Louis XII and was therefore untouchable; the Colonna, the count of Pitigliano and Bartolomeo d'Alviano were already employed either by Venice or by Spain.

The idea of having a native force permanently in readiness, which could be supplemented in case of need by hired mercenaries but could defend Florence on their own had been mooted before. It was with his own troops that Florentine dominion had been won two centuries before. There were contemporary examples. The famous Swiss infantry learned their craft on parades in their village squares, went off to war along with their neighbours, and returned to their homes until the next alarm. When Alexander VI asked the Baglioni of Perugia to help Cesare Borgia take Camerino, Giampaolo Baglioni called out the able-bodied citizens in arms. And Cesare Borgia himself had used the traditional levy of one man per household to create a practicable trained force, licked into shape by the violent Spaniard, don Michele Coriglia. But Florence was a peaceable, commercial city, very different from the warlike towns of central Italy. She was ruled not by professional soldiers but by merchants and landowners. She was, moreover, fearful that if the subject towns were armed they would revolt, that if the people of the country were made into soldiers they would turn against their exploiters in the city. Reluctant to give any citizen more authority than others, the Florentines were afraid that Soderini might use the militia for his own private ends. The use of mercenaries eked out with irregulars had been inefficient from a military, but it had been at least safe from a political, point of view.

Matters were complicated in 1505 by the rapid growth of opposition to Soderini. Although his period of office had seen a greater stability in both internal and foreign policies and a considerable improvement in the finances of the city, he was inevitably suspected of personal ambition. His skill in by-passing opposition was noted against him; the marriage of a great-nephew to a grand-niece of Lorenzo di Pierfrancesco dei Medici was another straw in the wind. He was believed to be nourishing an element in the public service that was more loyal to him personally than to the constitution as a whole, an element of which Machiavelli was known to be part.

Soderini therefore had the militia project approved by the Council of Eighty and then stood aside, leaving the organization to Machiavelli, who was to produce a working model, as it were, and show that it was not only efficient but innocuous. Recruiting was to take place in the country districts of Tuscan Romagna, Casentino, and Mugello, and after local training on the Swiss model, the men were to be paraded in Florence itself to show the steadiness of their discipline.

The choice of Machiavelli was an obvious one. He had been more and more closely concerned with the military side of his department's business since 1499, and had been pressing for a militia at least since 1503, when he discussed it with Cardinal Soderini in Rome. From December 1505 until the following April he was engaged in putting the scheme into effect. He went from one local authority to another instructing them to raise men and planning the administrative units into which they were to be grouped. The work was full of annoyances. On February 5th he wrote from Pontassieve, near Vallombrosa: 'Two causes have contributed to give me the greatest trouble in this matter; the one is the inveterate habit of disobedience of these people, and the other is the enmity existing between the people of Petrognano and those of Campana, who live on either side of the mountain.' When he enrolled the men of Campana, the men of Petrognano refused to have anything to do with the scheme. He was hampered by the happy-go-lucky methods of local mayors, and their tendency to look upon militia service not (as Machiavelli tried to present it) as a privilege but as an imposition for which they could drive a hard bargain. 'I have not been able to complete this business with greater dispatch,' he wrote on the same occasion, 'and if anyone thinks differently, let him try, and he will find out what it is to bring together a lot of peasants like these.' But by February 15th he was able to produce a first parade in Florence, and its publicity value can be judged from the diarist Luca Landucci's enthusiastic description. 'There was a muster in the Piazza [della Signoria] of 400 recruits whom the gonfalioner had assembled, Florentine peasants, and he gave them each a white waistcoat, a pair of stockings, half red and half white, a white cap, shoes, and an iron breastplate and lances, and to some of them arquebuses. They were soldiers, but lived in their own houses, being obliged to appear when needed, and it was ordered that many thousands should be made in this way through the country, so that we should not need any foreigners. This was thought the finest thing that had ever been arranged for Florence.'

The aim was to elaborate the scheme until not less than ten thousand men were available at any time. Lists were compiled of all males over fifteen years by the local mayors or rectors, and those actually chosen for enrolment were chosen from the men between eighteen and thirty. Those without arms were given them. Some units were to be entirely composed of arquebusiers, but in every unit one man in ten was to be armed with a gun. Service involved certain privileges : exemption from any fines then outstanding for criminal charges, and permission to carry arms in towns—in Florence even in the Palazzo della Signoria itself, a risky provision, but thought a good advertisement for the steady morale of the troops. For every ten men there was a corporal. Each company (or *bandiera*) comprised from one to three hundred men and was commanded by a captain with a drummer to help him in giving orders. Several companies—the men of one province, or valley, together—formed a battalion, and this was commanded by a constable, himself a professional soldier; usually, but not necessarily, a Florentine subject.

The men were drilled on each holiday, and twice a year a general reunion was held in each provincial centre. These were often attended by someone from headquarters, Machiavelli himself, or Giacomini, for instance. Mass was held in public, and this was followed by a harangue on the duties of the militia and on the love of country and of liberty. The parade proper then began, with orders and formations based on Swiss

models. Discipline was, in theory, fierce. Desertion was
punished by death, and failure to enrol or to turn up
on parade might lead to the culprit being taken before
the military authorities in Florence. At the other end
of the scale, there was to be no swearing or gaming or
quarrelling. There were two contrasting aids to discipline. In every local centre a drum-shaped box was
hung in the main church which was painted with a
figure of Saint John (the patron of Florence) and the
words *Tamburo d'Ordinanza*, and into this a denun-
ciation of any crime that concerned the militia could
be slipped. The other aid was provided by the formidable Don Michele, the professional soldier who had
acquired a reputation for great harshness under Cesare
Borgia; he rode round from parade to parade with a
squad of fifty foot and thirty horse to watch out for
any irregularity, and was permitted to inflict penalties
including torture but on the hither side of death.

There was a formidable amount of paper work involved. The constable had to keep the following
records: men enrolled as capable of bearing arms;
men capable but not yet enrolled; men by platoons,
under each corporal; men struck off the roll, showing
why and what had become of their arms; those still
requiring arms, and why, showing losses, etc.; arms
held by the constable; offenders. These records were
kept with the assistance of a secretary, and one of
Machiavelli's duties was to check them on his tours of
inspection.

All this organization was ratified in December 1506,
and put in the charge of a new department, the Nine
of the Militia, after Machiavelli had produced a report based on his experience to date and suggesting the

lines on which the militia should be run in future. This *Discourse on Florentine Military Preparation* begins with the general proposition that states and their rulers depend on two things—justice and arms. Florence has little justice and no arms, but both order and strength can be regained if the city determines on a national militia. He agrees that it would be better to avoid arming the subject cities and restrict recruiting to the rural areas because the humour of Tuscany is such that 'he who once learned to live independently would never again want a master'. Apart from practical details of numbers, the hierarchy of command, parades and the like, a good deal of the report is taken up with further political safeguards. These reflect the precautions built into the Florentine constitution itself against a concentration of power in a few hands, and were put in to quench any fears that the militia might turn on its master.

An attempt should be made in the first place 'to infuse it with some religious principles in order to make it more obedient'. This was catered for by the public masses and harangues and the *tamburi* hung solemnly in churches. To prevent a monopoly of authority within Florence itself there should be a division of function; the militia should be organized by one body (it was to be the Nine), commanded by another, the Ten, and paid by yet another. The constables should not be put over men from their own districts, but a constable from Casentino should command men from the Mugello, and so forth, and their commands should change from year to year so that they did not build up a dangerous influence over their men. All the companies should serve under the same device, the Mar-

zocco, or Lion of Florence, so that they should be aware
that they had no provincial but only a public loyalty.
With these safeguards, he concluded : 'You will see in
your own day the difference between having your
fellow citizens soldiers by choice, not by corruption, as
they are at present.' When the Nine were appointed,
Machiavelli was made their Chancellor, while remaining Second Chancellor and secretary of the Ten. In
time of war control of the militia was to pass from the
Nine to the Ten. Cardinal Soderini wrote enthusiastic-
ally from Rome on the 15th, when the news reached
him. 'This measure surely *sit a Deo* . . . the city has
done nothing so honourable and secure for a long
time'; and writing later, on March 4th, he referred to
the militia again. 'Your pleasure cannot be small, since
it was your hand that gave a start to such a worthy
business'.

During the late summer of 1506 Machiavelli was
taken away from his militia duties to go on a mission to
the Pope. Julius II had at last matured his plans for a
resumption of papal territories in central Italy, and left
Rome on August 26th with a small force to take
Perugia and Bologna, hoping that French aid would
reach him on the way. He had asked for a force from
the mercenaries employed by Florence, and Machiavelli's instructions were to agree to this, but to make
excuses for putting off any action for as long as possible. Julius was still a dark horse, and Florence was
hesitant to back him. The main interest in this second
mission to the papal court lies on the one hand in
tracing Machiavelli's growing admiration for Julius,
and on the other his own growing self-assurance. Writing from Viterbo on September 2nd, he spoke of Julius

disparagingly : 'Those who know the Pope say that with him one cannot place a thing overnight and find it there the next day.' But as the court moved north he saw the Pope's fixity of purpose, and his unscrupulous determination to achieve it, slowly unfolding. On reaching Perugia, where Giampaolo Baglioni remained in full military command, Machiavelli filled a dispatch with a splendidly reasoned account of why the Pope would probably shelve the problem of its possession until a later and better-provided day. Julius, however, at the risk of his liberty and quite possibly his life, entered Perugia and obtained Giampaolo's submission. French aid was still not forthcoming, but Julius did not hesitate to press on towards Bologna. It was at this juncture, at Cesena, that, as Machiavelli described in a dispatch of October 3rd, ambassadors came from Bologna to remind Julius of the treaties made by former popes with their city and confirmed by himself. 'His Holiness replied that . . . as to the treaties, he cared neither for those made by other popes, nor for that made by himself, for neither his predecessors nor himself could have done otherwise, and that it was necessity and not his free will that had made him confirm the treaty; but that the time had now arrived for correcting these things, and it seemed to him that if he did not do so he would have no excuse to offer to the Almighty.' And Machiavelli added ; 'The ambassadors remained confounded, and after a few words of reply they took their leave.' After witnessing this scene, it is not surprising to find Machiavelli writing from Palazzuolo on October 19th : 'Everybody here is of the opinion that, if the Pope succeeds in his attempt upon Bologna, he will lose no time in engaging in more important enterprises, and it is thought that now or never will Italy be relieved of those who have plotted to devour her.' The Pope did succeed. The expected French aid arrived, and on November 11th he entered Bologna and set about reforming its government.

Machiavelli was relieved on October 27th. Letters from Buonaccorsi [1] had kept him in touch with family news and official gossip, of which the most unpleasant item was that Alamanno Salviati had been heard to say of him at a dinner party, 'I will trust that scoundrel with nothing when I am on the Ten'; a remark showing that Salviati was more affected by Machiavelli's connection with Soderini than by receiving the dedication of *The First Decade*. More encouraging news was given of the militia, though the work involved was sorely needing his presence.

The success of this important scheme doubtless played its part in strengthening the note of assurance that had entered Machiavelli's official correspondence. At the age of thirty-seven, with eight years' chancery experience and with friends in high places, he had become an influential, though still a subordinate, figure in government circles. His dispatches, from the first mission to the papal court in 1503 to this second mission in 1506, reflect his increased confidence. Before, though never less than competent, they had been a little defensive, a shade hair-splitting and arbitrary, at times a little shrill. After 1503 they are crisp, pungent and easy; he improvises and elaborates freely, while remaining in line with the instructions of the

[1] Machiavelli was so much on the move that Buonaccorsi was sometimes in doubt where to send them. On October 10th he addressed one to Machiavelli 'At Forlì, or wherever the devil he is.'

Ten. His criticisms of his own government become increasingly forthright. Though his style remains clear and without flourishes, it becomes more relaxed, and he allows himself a freer use of literary allusions and proverbial expressions. There is even a note of ruling-class mentality in his impatient references to the temperament and political views of the masses. He was always abundantly busy. With the intention of maintaining the historiographical traditions of his department, he had begun accumulating notes for a history of Florence from the middle of the previous century, but had had no time to bring them into shape. History was being made faster than a secretary of the Ten could record it. The breathing space was nearly over; in 1507 the forebodings of *The First Decade* were realized as Italy became once more the subject of barbarian interest—French, Spanish, and German.

CHAPTER FIVE

The German Mission and the Fall of Pisa: 1507 – 1509

THE spring of 1507 was taken up for Machiavelli by continued militia business : supplying local recruiting centres with money and arms, deciding whether breaches of discipline could be settled on the spot or required a visit from Don Michele, selecting captains, and preventing trained militiamen from being counter-recruited by professional free companies. Italy meanwhile was slowly filling with the repercussions of an isolated civil revolt in Genoa in the previous winter, where the popular party, expelling their aristocratic rulers, had appealed for aid to Maximilian, while the aggrieved *grandi* turned to France. In April Louis XII entered Italy with an army and in person restored them, thus antagonizing Maximilian whose old resolve to assert his power in Italy and be crowned at Rome was roused from its long torpor.

When this was known in Florence, party tension increased as it had when Maximilian's descent had last been mooted in 1502. Soderini's supporters maintained that nothing should be done to imperil the French alliance, on which their recovery of Pisa depended, while his opponents pressed for closer relations with Germany. As usual, little was known about the Emperor's precise intentions, nor about the likely reactions of the other Italian states. When news came that Julius was sending a legate, Bernardino Carvajal, to Germany therefore, Florence clutched at this straw. Machiavelli was sent to intercept him on his way north at Siena, to learn how seriously the Pope was taking Maximilian's plans, and to gauge by the nature of the reception given the legate by the Sienese at what level Florence should pitch her own.

The pettifogging nature of the mission shows that Machiavelli, for all his talents and experience, retained his factotum status. He counted the number of horses and mules in the legate's equippage as they entered the town; he found out where the retinue was being lodged, and at what cost; he weighed the diplomatic significance of the presents offered by the city fathers: two barrels of mulberries, three baskets of large pigeons, each containing five pairs, etc. 'From what I hear', he reported on August 10th, 'the people of this city will make a great holiday of the Emperor's arrival, which is desired by all.' And referring to the contrast between Petrucci's ostensible friendship for Florence and the affection of his subjects for the Pisans, whom it was thought Maximilian wished to help, he added : 'I mention this to your Lordships, as in matters of this kind the will of the people generally differs from that of its chiefs.'

This nervous concern to discover current attitudes towards Maximilian is all the more interesting in that Florence had already a representative at the emperor's court. Maximilian's secrecy, the ignorance that prevailed in Italy about the internal condition of Germany, and the reluctance of the government to come to a decision on this point, all resulted in a jumpy and distrustful atmosphere at home. The election of the representative had illustrated this. Soderini had proposed to send Machiavelli, as someone on whom he could rely, but as Machiavelli was making his preparations to leave there were complaints from Soderini's opponents. Why should he send one of 'his' men, a departmental official, when there were young *uomini da bene*, the very group from whom future ambassadors should be chosen for training, standing idle? As a result, Soderini was forced to give in and Francesco Vettori was sent instead. He was thirty-three, five years Machiavelli's junior, and this was his first diplomatic mission. As his dispatch was a preliminary move, a fact-finding probe rather than a negotiation, he was sent with the non-committal rank of mandatory.

The next question to settle was whether ambassadors should be sent as well. Soderini, not wanting to be committed to a formal relationship with Maximilian, opposed the idea, but his opponents forced it through, and two ambassadors were elected, one of them being his foremost critic, Alamanno Salviati. Nor was this the end: were the ambassadors now chosen actually to be sent? Again there were two conflicting opinions. Soderini's supporters thought that Maximilian could not rely on widespread help from the German princes and cities, and that he was not therefore a danger; better, then, to stick to France, who certainly was. His opponents read the evidence contrariwise, and as the debate grew warm accused him of clinging to France for personal reasons; it was pointed out that his brother the cardinal enjoyed a lucrative income from benefices in France. The struggle was prolonged and

bitter. The information available to both sides was
scant and could bear varying interpretations; in fact,
though Florence's German policy was the subject
under discussion, the larger issue involved was whether
the government should or should not be changed. The
matter reached a deadlock; as a compromise it was
decided to send no ambassadors but a second mandatory, and Soderini's influence was still great enough
to make the choice fall on Machiavelli, who left
Florence on December 17th and had got as far as
Geneva by Christmas Day.

It was soon clear how far Florentine foreign policy
was hampered by lack of knowledge about the northern countries. Both France and Germany were wooing
Switzerland for aid : to estimate which would win, it
was necessary to know how such decisions were reached
in Switzerland, and their binding force. But Machiavelli, writing from Bolzano on January 17th, was reduced to this sort of remark : 'I have learned from
various persons, but mainly from a gentleman at
Fribourg, a very accurate man, . . . that the main body
of this country consists of twelve communities leagued
together, and called cantons, the names of which
are . . .' and he gives them. To discuss accurate news
about the Emperor was impossible. He tried to find
what forces and money Maximilian was in command
of. He asked the duke of Savoy's ambassador ('a man
who is sixty years of age, and generally esteemed as a
prudent man') what he thought on this score, only to
be answered : 'You want to know in two hours what I
have not been able to learn in many months.' Machiavelli was soon to learn the force of this gloomy re-
joinder. Meanwhile, he reported that he had heard

many reports of troop movements, but added that 'this is all I have heard, but what I have seen is, that from Geneva to Memmingen, throughout the many miles I have travelled, I have not seen a single mounted man or foot soldier. True, in the neighbourhood of Constance, in some of the places off the road I heard some drumming, and was told by some that it came from remnants of infantry that had stopped there, but others said that it was peasants merrymaking.' Vettori, in a dispatch written on the same day, confessed to a similar difficulty. The Florentine government had at length agreed to give Maximilian a sum of money in return for his protection. It was to be paid, however, in three instalments; the first when he reached a city that was 'wholly Italian', the second on entering Tuscan territory, the third three months later, or, better still, when he actually arrived at Rome. In this way Florence would not be out of pocket if the danger were not to be materialized. Maximilian was thought to be aiming towards Trent, and Vettori explained that : 'As you charge me to make the first payment only when the Emperor with his army shall have arrived at a city wholly upon Italian soil, I am discreetly endeavouring to find out the exact position of Trent. The people of the country tell me that the boundary line between Italy and Germany runs more than a mile to this side.'

It was a most uncomfortable mission for both the mandatories. Their instructions were to offer money, but only to conclude an agreement if they were quite sure that Maximilian would enter Italy with an army. It was precisely this last point that was so difficult; no one appeared to have any clear idea not only of Maximilian's plans but the degree of backing he would get

from Germany in carrying them out. He disliked
having ambassadors around him, and made them all
stay at some distance from the court. This lack of
knowledge on the spot was paralleled by a lack of fresh,
clear instructions from home. Communications were
difficult because of the uneasy state of the border;
letters from home were rare and avidly waited for.
Disappointment followed disappointment. On one
occasion a messenger had destroyed all his papers when
interrogated in crossing Lombardy, on another the
courier had concealed his letter so long in his shoe that
it turned out to be illegible; on yet a third, a dispatch
reached Vettori and Machiavelli in a loaf of bread
'where it had become first wet and then dry; it could
only be got out in pieces, and consequently', grieved
Vettori, 'I could not read more than one fourth of it, and
that in disconnected sentences'. To add to their difficulties, the Florentine policy, such as it was, was exceedingly hard to carry out, requiring important
decisions to be carried out in terms of nebulous data.
'Be it said with the utmost respect,' Vettori was moved
to protest on May 30th, 'your Lordships have spun this
thread so fine that it is impossible to weave it.'

The dispatches of this mission were signed by Vettori, and some passages including some of the tediously
composed code paragraphs, were in his hand. But
Machiavelli, as was suitable in a chancery official,
wrote most of them out on lines which Vettori and he
had probably discussed between them. Vettori was in
charge of the mission. Machiavelli was there as his
secretary and information-gatherer; but Vettori was
obviously glad to have an experienced colleague, and
asked that Machiavelli should be allowed to stay on.

It is seldom profitable to distinguish between the opinions of the two men. They had much in common, and the friendship begun on this mission lasted for the rest of Machiavelli's life. Vettori was a man of letters —his *Travels in Germany* was based on this experience—and his literary style, as we know from their letters five years later, is not always easy to tell from Machiavelli's own.

For Machiavelli the mission lasted nearly five months. The nearest Maximilian got to entering Italy was some desultory warfare in Friuli which ended with his signing an inglorious truce with Venice on June 6th. Soderini's forecast had been correct : the combination of Maximilian's own erratic nature and the half-hearted support he was given meant that the German danger was less grave than had been feared. Machiavelli left Trent on June 10th and returned to Florence on the 16th. This was his only personal contact with Switzerland and Germany, and in spite of his long absence from Florence, he had seen very little of them. He had crossed Switzerland quickly, and in Germany he hardly moved out of the Tyrol—Innsbruck, Bolzano, and Trent being the centres he spent most time in. He spoke no German, and had to rely on the information given him by educated Latin-speaking or Italian-speaking Germans at the court. For all this, perhaps because of it, Machiavelli returned with strong and lasting impressions.

He wrote three accounts of Germany. The *Report on Germany* was written on the day after his return to Florence. The *Discourse on Germany and the Emperor* was written when ambassadors were going to Germany in 1509. It refers to the *Report* and does not supplement the views or information given there. The *Description of German Affairs* was written at some unspecified time after April 11th, 1512, for the battle of Ravenna, fought on that day, is mentioned. It is a more literary presentation of much the same material as he used in the *Report*, omitting only the *Report*'s admirable portrait of the kindly, disorganized, inefficient Maximilian, secretive and yet dependent on his advisers. On the other hand the *Description* shows the enduring influence of his admiration for the military and social virtues of—he calls them Germans, generalizing from the Tyrol and incorporating Swiss features as well. It falls into three sections : why Germany is strong ; why this strength cannot be utilized; in what the merit of German troops consists. It is tempting to see him using a somewhat idealized Germany as a stalking-horse for an attack on the errors of his fellow citizens : their persistence in relying too much on mercenaries, their love of display and their reluctance to pay taxes. German strength is firmly rooted in arms, he claims—arms born by citizens. Germans are modest and unostentatious, and their states are thrifty and cautious, not grudging others what they themselves do not need. Moreover, they are provident. They anticipate trouble wisely and do not fleet carelessly from moment to moment. Crisis finds them armed to meet it. In the second part he explains why this potential strength cannot be readily mobilized because of mutual rivalries : city against city, cities against princes, princes against one another, and all against the Emperor. He cites 1508 as an illustration. The third section is a technical description of the German cavalry and infantry, with reasons for the superiority of the latter. In all these German writings Machiavelli is content with a narrow range of information. He was concerned as a government official to discuss Germany's war potential, and as a propagandist, to splash a German coat of paint on his particular hobby-horses, the advantages of national troops and the evil effects of hesitant, divided authority, stressing by implication the contrast between Germany and the efficiently centralized France.

On the Pisan front matters had hung fire, but a blockade was put into operation as soon as possible in the following year which was the first with any pretensions to be total. Sophisticated methods like undermining the defenders' morale by propaganda were ignored; this was to be a simple throttling strategy. Every route that cunning or desperation could find in and out of Pisa was to be stopped. Access from the sea up the Arno had been stopped in the previous autumn by a barrier at San Pietro in Grado, but supplies had continued to come up the Fiume Morto and thence into Pisa via the Osoli. A barrier was therefore constructed across the Fiume Morto, protected by a strong-point and controlled by men from San Pietro in Grado. A camp was established at San Iacopo in the valley of the Serchio, cutting off communications with

---

[1] The *Description of French Affairs* was possibly written for a similar purpose as the *Discourse*. It contains far more detailed and statistical information than any of the writings on Germany, and it is not like to have been written after Machiavelli's dismissal deprived him of the use of official documents. On the other hand he mentions the battle of Ravenna. This suggests a date between that battle (April 11th, 1512) and November 1512; certainly before August 1513, the date of the battle of the Spurs, for Machiavelli says of the English that 'none of the people now living has ever seen the face of an enemy'.

Lucca via Librafatta, and a third camp at Mezzana guarded the Val di Calci. Each camp was garrisoned with a thousand infantry and a cavalry force. Machiavelli was back there in February 1509. Though operations were actually in the care of the commissary at Cascina, Niccolò Capponi, Machiavelli, as Soderini's personal representative, had a roving commission which brought him a large share of responsibility. It was, after all, a spade-and-shovel operation. As well as keeping a continual eye on the militia, who comprised more than two-thirds of the infantry at the camps, he was in charge of the Arno and Fiume Morto obstructions, and with making a practicable ford across the Osoli for the Florentine troops. He moved between the camps dealing with food supplies, pay, and applications for sick leave. The militia, though he declared them 'splendid', provided some headaches. Writing from Molina di Quosa on March 7th, he explained that he would have to reduce the strength of their companies by two-thirds for a while, as the season was approaching when the silkworm needed special attention at home.

In bantering recognition of his multiple duties Buonaccorsi wrote a letter from Florence on February 20th addressed to *Magnifice generalis capitaneus*, etc., and by March the number of men, troops, and labourers had grown so large that more commissaries were sent. Nor had Machiavelli had only his military duties. On March 4th he was sent to Lucca to complain of infringements of an agreement not to send supplies to Pisa, and on the 10th he was sent to Piombino to investigate an offer of some Pisan citizens to negotiate with Florence under the auspices of Iacopo d'Appiano. The Ten suspected this, rightly, of being a device to waste time, and were unwilling to move until Machiavelli had investigated it. In a few days he was back among the camps again. On April 14th he was ordered to remain at Cascina, to collect ammunition there. 'That post', he protested at once, 'can be filled by any man, no matter of what qualifications; whilst if I remained there I could no longer be of any service to the army here, nor be in any other way of use. I am aware that this post would expose me to less danger and fatigue, but if I wanted to avoid danger and fatigue I should not have left Florence. And therefore I entreat your Lordships to allow me to remain in the camps to co-operate with the commissaries in all measures that have to be taken.' And he concludes : 'For here I can make myself useful, but at Cascina I should not be good for anything, and should die of sheer desperation.' He was soon on the move again, moving from camp to camp, helping compose difficulties, aiding with blockade arrangements, dealing with supply bottlenecks. As symbol of his manifold interests he received from time to time in camp letters from the Ten in Florence (whose secretary he remained) signed in the course of routine with his own name.

The noose was now about the city's neck: it was just a question of keeping it tight until the citizens gasped for surrender. And this year there was no one to intervene and help them. In Lombardy a European conflict was in progress : none of the contestants was concerned for the issue of a domestic side-show on the western edge of Tuscany. The Pisans were the almost accidental casualties of a war which forced Venice back to her lagoons. In December 1508 the league of Cambrai had been formed between Louis XII, Maximilian and Ferdinand of Aragon largely at the prompting of Julius II, who became a party to it. His aim was to recover for the Church from Venice the triangle of territory Faenza–Ravenna–Rimini. The remaining possessions of Venice were to go to the other parties : the Lombard provinces west of Lake Garda to France, those to the east, including Friuli, to Maximilian.

Ferdinand was to get the Venetian possessions, like Brindisi and Otranto, in the kingdom of Naples. He was to attack by sea, the others by land. The League was first explained as a great crusading scheme, but in the spring of 1509 it was clear that an offensive was being mounted against Venice. Julius excommunicated the city on April 27th, and the French army began to move east from Milan ten days later. It met the Venetian army at Agnadello, just across the Adda, on May 14th and routed it, leaving Venice helpless before any advance the allies chose to make. When the news was received in Florence, Landucci noted, 'there were great rejoicings with bonfires', and Florence had some cause, indeed, to be pleased by the humiliation of a rival who had been a consistent supporter of Pisa. But it is a significant indication of the narrowness of Florence's outlook on foreign affairs, that her dislike of Venice, which Machiavelli abundantly shared, could stomach the partition of Italian soil among foreign powers.

It was in the month of Agnadello that the Pisans finally sued for peace on the terms that Florence offered of unconditional surrender but with a promise of merciful treatment. Machiavelli wrote to the Ten on May 20th announcing the arrival of Pisan citizens to arrange a safe conduct for their ambassadors, and he remained in close touch with the peace negotiations, accompanying the ambassador to Florence and when the agreement was concluded, entering Pisa on June 8th with a detachment of his militia—who had been given an advance of pay to dissuade them from looting. Machiavelli received full credit for the role of the militia in the conclusion of this long operation, and he

was widely congratulated by his friends, one of them,
Filippo da Casavecchia, himself a war commissary,
referring to the great part Machiavelli had played in
the victory, and saying that his militia project had
shown him to be 'a greater prophet than the Jews or
any other generation ever possessed'. On the other
hand, those who thought that Soderini's *mannerino*,[1]
or puppet, was getting above himself were surer of this
than ever. It did not escape Alamanno Salviati that he,
a commissary, had less influence over the militia than
Machiavelli, letter-writer and factotum to the Ten.
And if Machiavelli's career had become less secure by
becoming more conspicuous, the success of the militia
was itself a danger for Florence. Its troops had been
used, but they had not been tested. They had barred
the roads, but they had not had to stop anyone getting
through. Pisa had fallen by blockade, not assault. The
usefulness of the militia, the energy of the Pisans themselves in defeating siege after siege, the success with
which citizen soldiers were to defend Padua against
Maximilian's huge siege train after its recapture by the
Venetians in July, were all factors which blended, in
the minds of Machiavelli and Soderini, into too great
a reliance on non-professional troops.

The fact that the war of the League had at last
brought Maximilian into Italy meant that the money
promised by Machiavelli and Vettori in the previous
year had actually to be paid, and in November
Machiavelli was sent to Mantua to hand over the
second instalment. He was then to continue a free-
lance investigation into the progress of the war against

[1] The word was reported by the contemporary Florentine
historian Cerretani.

Venice at Verona—'or wherever it may seem more convenient to you to obtain more precise information on the subject'. Verona was suggested because it became the headquarters of the imperial army after Maximilian had raised his fruitless siege of Padua. The Venetians had made good use of the slackening interest in the war shown by France and Julius II after these rulers had seized their own prizes, and began the recapture of Maximilian's share, first Treviso, then Padua, then, as Machiavelli heard on reaching Mantua, Vicenza. There had been some fierce guerrilla resistance to the invaders on the part of the local peasantry—another vindication of the militia principle —and Venice had learned a Machiavellian lesson, for as he told the Ten in a dispatch from Verona on December 7th, 'in all the places of which the Venetians make themselves the masters, they cause the image of St. Mark to be painted, but with a sword in hand instead of a book; from which it would seem that they have learned to their cost that books and study do not suffice for the protection of states'.

He remained at Verona for some three weeks, while slow winter skirmishing made the countryside unsafe without producing any notable advantage to either side. The city was troubled by differences between the French and German troops quartered there, and once there was a false alarm which gave Machiavelli a chance of counting the soldiers as they formed up in the streets; but on the whole it was a quiet time, and Machiavelli was able to turn diplomatic idleness to literary advantage. It is possible that it was here that he began a continuation to *The First Decade*. Five years had passed since this was finished, and the whole ten would be a long time to wait before carrying the story forward. The result, known as *The Second Decade,* takes it up to the Venetian reoccupation of Vicenza. It is less than half the length of *The First Decade*, and its verse is more mechanical, the flashes of wit and feeling fewer. There are only two passages of sustained fervour. One is an encomium on Giacomini, the other is an exhortation to the Italian states to learn from the collapse of Venice at Agnadello before it was too late : heaven smites as fast as the seasons change— 'if your prudence were devoted to recognizing the danger, and remedying it, then heaven would no longer have such power'. There is nothing of the cautious mandatory vainly scanning the morrow's sky in his scorn of those 'who possess crowns and sceptres and know nothing of the future !'; no inhibiting thought of the Pisan war in his reproach : 'You are blinded so much by your present greed that you have a thick veil over your eyes and cannot see things that are far off'. In Machiavelli the excitement of literary composition, working on a dogmatic and sanguine nature, could produce remarks that defied his own experience.

He had time for correspondence, and one at least of his letters was a *novella* in all but name. In it he caps an amorous adventure told him by Luigi Guicciardini with a grotesque encounter which he claims had befallen him. Luigi's story had presumably been one of successful love; Machiavelli's in sardonic contrast, was a calamitous tale of lust. He describes his being introduced by a 'laundress' to a prostitute in a dimly lit room. All would have been well if he had not insisted on lighting a lamp to see what she looked like. As it was, the lamp nearly fell from his hand before it was properly lit.

'Ugh! I nearly fell dead on the spot, she was so ugly. The first thing I saw was a tuft of hair, half white, half black, piebald, that is, with age, and although the crown of her head was bald—which baldness enabled one to see a louse or two taking a stroll—still a few sparse hairs mingled with the whiskers sprouting round her face; and on top of her meagre and wrinkled head was a fiery scar which made her look as if she had been branded in the market. There were colonies of nits in each eyebrow; one eye looked up, the other down, and one was larger than the other; the tear ducts were full of rheum, the rims hairless. Her nose was screwed into her face at an angle, the nostrils full of snot, and one of them was half missing; her mouth was like Lorenzo dei Medici's, but twisted up on one side, and it drooled a little : as she had no teeth she could not keep her saliva in. Her upper lip had a scant but fairly lengthy moustache. Her chin was long and sharp, pointing up a little, whence a scanty dewlap dangled to her Adam's apple.

This description, which in the original marvellously exemplifies the way in which the nutcracker-like grip of Machiavelli's prose style breaks a situation into hard, sharp, definite splinters, was written on December 8th. On November 30th Buonaccorsi had written a short note from Florence giving Machiavelli the names of the newly elected Ten. He followed this a month later, on December 27th, with a letter addressed 'Ubi Sit', designed to catch Machiavelli on his way back to Florence. It contained a warning that an attempt had been made to get him dismissed from office on the ground that his father had died in debt to the state;

strictly speaking, this was a disqualification for state employment, but to disinter the information in order to ruin an eleven-year-long career was the product of pure malice. The attempt had failed, but Buonaccorsi reported that he was distressed by the little support there was forthcoming for Machiavelli. The affair in fact blew over, and Machiavelli settled back into office a few days later; but it was an indication of the dangers involved in being Soderini's *mannerino*.

CHAPTER SIX

Defeat and Dismissal: 1510 – 1512

WHILE Machiavelli spent the spring of 1510 engaged in militia business, the shape of international politics was undergoing a drastic revision in the face of Julius II's change of front: perturbed by the foothold France and Maximilian had gained in Lombardy, and, satisfied by his own acquisitions, he began to substitute for his former 'Down with Venice!' 'Out with the Barbarians!'—a cry that was to become notorious. In February he signed peace terms with the Venetians and prepared a three-pronged assault on his ex-ally, France, aiming at Ferrara and Genoa, both French dependencies, and urging the Swiss to invade Lombardy from the north.

Florence was in a delicate position, caught between two traditional friendships. Apart from the Savonarolan interlude, she had been friendly towards the papacy: from 1494 she had remained an ally of France. Her best friends were now at one another's throats: which should she help? To gain time, Soderini sent Machiavelli to Louis on June 24th. He was to say that Florence hoped an open rupture between France and the papacy could be avoided, and to urge Louis to continue the war against Venice. But Machiavelli found Louis resolutely anti-papal and preparing a general council of the Church which would depose

Julius II. He commented on these plans in a dispatch of August 18th; 'In truth, if your Lordships were situated elsewhere, all this would be very desirable, so that our priests might also taste a little of the bitterness of this world.' Florence, however, was not in a position to be detached; a decision had to be made and Machiavelli was anxious that she should take the side of the French.

As seen from Louis's court, the danger from Julius did not seem, after all, so very great. The attack on Genoa failed and Louis was not seriously perturbed by the danger to Milan from the Swiss, whose Confederation was playing an increasingly important role in European politics. Machiavelli quoted him on July 26th as saying: 'By my faith, I am in doubt whether to let them pass or not, for I do not know whether it would be better that the Pope should be unarmed, or that he should have armour on his back that will hurt him'—a reference to the unreliability of the Swiss as employees—and on August 9th he wrote to urge a whole-hearted support of the king. As possible rewards, Lucca and Urbino had been hinted at, 'If you think it well to risk your fortune with that of France, you will be able to dispose of a good part of Tuscany as you choose.' This suggestion had all the more force in that central Italy was constantly the scene of projected unions; Machiavelli had referred to a French scheme in 1500 to join Pisa, Pietrasanta, Livorno, Piombino, and Lucca; Louis had considered countering Cesare Borgia's empire with a league between Florence, Siena, Bologna, and Lucca in 1503. But not even the mention of Urbino could tempt Florence to get down from her fence, and when Machiavelli was relieved in September by his friend Roberto Acciaiuoli, she was still uncommitted to either side.

From Florence indeed Julius II looked more formidable. He had scored some successes in the drive against Ferrara, taking Cento (to the south-west) and besieging Mirandola, to the west, pressing the assault through the hard winter that brought the year to a close. While remaining diplomatically neutral, Florence was concerned for her own military position, and soon after his return on October 19th, Machiavelli was asked to look into the possibility of raising a cavalry militia—and to produce, as with the infantry, a test force to reassure any possible critics. To this end he spent November and December recruiting in the 'safe' rural districts. His idea was to have a force of light horsemen armed with lances or cross-bows or even arquebuses, which could be used for foraging and skirmish and reconnoitre. Heavy cavalry was expensive to arm and drill, and based as it was on the 'lance' unit of a man-at-arms with a number of mounted assistants and servants, it was really only suitable for a society of leisured nobles or for full-time professionals.

As might have been expected, Florence's neutrality was preserved at the price of growing domestic strain. On December 23rd a plot was discovered against Soderini's life. The would-be assassin, Prinzivalle della Stufa, had confided his plan to Filippo Strozzi, thinking that as Strozzi had in 1508 married—and it had caused some alarmed discussion at the time—Clarice dei Medici, a granddaughter of Lorenzo the Magnificent, he would favour a plot which might lead to the Medici's return. Instead, Strozzi denounced him and the plot foundered. At the end of December emergency provisions were passed, to ensure that the machinery of government was never interrupted long enough to make possible the calling of a *parlamento*— the classic Florentine device for effecting a change of régime. This measure, while reflecting the heat of party strife, was also calculated to feed it.

In the following year it became increasingly difficult for Florence to keep from declaring outright either for France or for the Pope. Julius began fortunately by storming Mirandola—in his impatience to enter he had himself lifted in through the breach on a litter without waiting for the gates to open—but it was his last forward move. The main factor in his recent successes had been the slackness of Chaumont, the French commander, and in February Chaumont was replaced by the veteran professional Trivulzio, and the young and impetuous Gaston de Foix. Julius was forced to withdraw to Bologna, and then to Ravenna with the French after him. The failure of Julius's thrust against Ferrara was demonstrated with cruel symbolism when the duke of Ferrara procured Michelangelo's statue of the Pope, which had been placed over the door of S. Antonio in Bologna, and had it melted down into a gun. When Julius returned to Rome at the end of May, he had lost all the territories taken from Ferrara, and was confronted by a new threat that carried the war to the very heart of his power : a general council was announced under French protection, and he was cited to appear before it at Pisa.

Florence continued to compensate for a waiting, and possibly dangerous, diplomatic game, by improving internal security. In the spring, Machiavelli was not only

sent out to recruit more light horse, but was given a
new duty : the inspection of fortresses. On January 5th
he went to Pisa with the engineer and architect Giuliano da Sangallo to report on the condition of the
citadel. On the 14th he went to Arezzo, and on February 15th to Poggio Imperiale for the same purpose. In
March he was recruiting cavalry in the upper Val
d'Arno and in Val di Chiana, and in April brought a
trial company of one hundred horse to Florence, as
part of the long and cautious business of having the
cavalry militia officially constituted. On May 1st he
was sent to Siena to renew the truce with that city
whereby Florence guaranteed to protect the Petrucci
administration in return for Montepulciano, the small
town dominating the southern Val di Chiana, which
Siena had taken from Florence in 1495. Even this
small transaction was an aspect of Franco-Papal
rivalry, for Julius had exerted himself to see that
Florence obtained Montepulciano in order that she
would turn a deaf ear to French demands that the
General Council should be heard on her territory. On
May 5th Machiavelli was on the move again, this time
in the opposite direction—to Monaco—in order to
conclude a commercial treaty with its lord, Luciano
Grimaldi. August found him recruiting again in the
Val di Chiana and the Casentino.

The General Council had been called for September
1st at Pisa. It was an anachronistic weapon. Its
theoretic basis was that authority can be taken from
an erring pope by a council representing the whole
Christian community, which claimed to govern in his
place until it chose a more worthy successor. The question of the legitimacy of this claim had never been

satisfactorily worked out. In 1415 a General Council really had legislated for the whole Church and chosen a pope, but this success was due to a situation which was urgent beyond precedent; there were three men who claimed to be pope, and the practical, as well as the ideological difficulties produced by this situation persuaded men to use a machinery few of them really trusted. When it was set running later to deal with situations that fell just short of being desperate, it failed to work, and little resentment was felt when Pius II declared in 1460 that appeals to a General Council over the head of a pope were 'erroneous and detestable'. General Councils called by the pope himself were a different matter: the administration and doctrine of the Church had been largely shaped by such bodies and Julius was taking the obvious, though by then somewhat antiquarian, step when he countered the Pisan Council by calling a Council, the Fifth Lateran, of his own. Logically, too, he excommunicated and deposed the cardinals who supported the French plan, and placed Pisa and Florence under an interdict. At the same time he tried to arrange a vast anti-French and anti-Florentine league, based on Spanish and Venetian support.

The Council of Pisa makes little show as an episode in the history either of France or of the papacy. A spiritual weapon used for a political purpose, it was crippled by the obvious cynicism of the mixture and the smallness of its scale: only four cardinals could be persuaded to attend it. But to the Florentines, it was a source of acute embarrassment. The two fires between which they had been caught since Julius broke with the French after Cambrai were blazing nearer than ever. In an attempt at compromise, Machiavelli was sent on September 10th to intercept the pro-French cardinals, who were late in travelling to Pisa, and to persuade them from going any farther. He was then to hasten on to Milan and try to persuade the French viceroy there, Gaston de Foix, to change the *venue* of the council, and then to carry on at once to France with the same plea. Roberto Acciaiuoli, the Florentine ambassador resident in France, described an interview he and Machiavelli had with Louis at Blois, in which the king admitted that the council had never been more than a diplomatic feint, and said that he thought the Florentines were exaggerating the danger of war as a consequence of the Pope's enmity, and that it was impossible to prevent the council opening at Pisa, though it might, in the course of time, be moved elsewhere. As for the risk of war, he thought it inconsiderable, for he did not believe that Spain would take any part in it, his relations with that power being very friendly.

He said this on September 23rd. But in fact, on October 4th the Holy League was concluded, whereby Spain pledged its military support to the Pope, and ordered the Viceroy of Naples, Raymond de Cardona, to bring an army up into the Romagna. The published aim of the treaty was the enforcement of papal and Venetian claims in northern Italy, but the implicit aim was the total expulsion of the French. Meanwhile, the French continued to press forward with preparations for the council, sending the schismatic cardinals down to Pisa with an armed guard from Milan. Machiavelli arrived home in Florence on November 2nd, and was sent next day to Pisa with a detachment of soldiers and the mission of both protecting the cardinals as long as they were on Florentine soil, and of urging them to get off it as soon as possible. His arguments—or rather, their own conviction that the internal situation was deteriorating rapidly, and the realization that their presence was bitterly resented by the Pisans themselves—had enough weight to determine them to move to Milan, and on November 12th he returned to Florence.

In all this transaction, Florence had been running both with the hare and the hounds. In trying to prevent the Council meeting and then persuading the cardinals to leave, she had been placating Julius, but in forcing the Pisan authorities to allow the Council actually to begin its sessions, she had been fostering a *protégé* of France. And she angered Julius by raising money during the crisis by means of a sharp tax on ecclesiastics. And as always, pace in the making of decisions on foreign policy was slowed by party friction at home. Soderini's party was still identified with France, and the opposition to him was becoming more favourable to the Medici as Julius appeared increasingly to favour the exiled members of that family. Since the death of Piero in 1503, the Medici, indeed, appeared much less as bogy figures. The despotism of Lorenzo was not forgotten, nor was the ineptitude of Piero, but the peace and prosperity of their years was increasingly recalled, and became elevated very soon to a quasi-mythical status. The peaceful years before 1494 were looked back on with yearning, and that golden age had flourished under the auspices of the Medici.

Julius announced that Cardinal Giovanni dei Medici, Lorenzo the Magnificent's son, would be his legate at

Bologna when it was taken by the League, hoping in this way to encourage Soderini's rivals to see the Medici as the obvious alternative to their present régime. This possibility was a persuasive one, for Giovanni reproduced many of his father's better traits. He was a liberal patron of the arts, cultivated, mild, and approachable. He had recently acted, unofficially, as guide and adviser to Florentines in Rome who had dealings with the curia, and he had impressed them as a moderate man, showing no trace of authoritarianism. It seemed possible, with him in mind, to contemplate a return of the Medici without this involving treachery to the ideals of the republic. The Strozzi-Medici marriage of 1508 had shown that antipathy to the Medici was tending to decline, for Filippo was not punished with anything like the full rigour of the laws condemning marriage with the child of an exile and rebel, and this tendency was now increased by the appearance of the Medici among the forces of the League. In the eyes of the League, the return to power of the Medici was the only guarantee that Florence would finally leave the French alliance.

Hamstrung by indecision, Florence could only wait and watch. The League began the year by besieging Bologna, but were forced to withdraw with the approach of the French army. Brescia, which had revolted against French rule, was retaken and sacked with frightful thoroughness by de Foix. His army then moved south-east, pushing the forces of the League down to Ravenna, where they made a stand. The battle that resulted was one of the most significant of a battle-studded epoch. The rival armies were roughly equal in size, and Europe had not till then seen so

many combatants come together, nor so many dead
left behind. It was the first battle whose fortunes were
determined by the use of artillery. But it was not only
for logistic and technical reasons that Ravenna scored
itself into the imagination of contemporaries. Still more
notable was the clouded way in which its issue was
declared. It looked at first like a French victory : the
League had heavier casualties and was forced to withdraw. Florence lit victory bonfires and instructed her
agents abroad to take a firmer pro-French line. But
at the moment of victory de Foix had been killed, and
it soon appeared how much the allies lost from this.
The League army had retired in good order and was
still in being. French rule in Lombardy was threatened
by a descent of twenty thousand Swiss, France herself
was threatened with invasion by an English and
Spanish force. The French army had to withdraw to
save Milan, and the whole fabric of French conquest
rolled back after it : first Ravenna, then Bologna,
Parma, Piacenza, Bergamo, Peschiera ; they withdrew
past Milan itself, leaving only a garrison in the citadel,
back to Asti, back to France itself. Florence, with the
bonfires of rejoicing scarcely quenched, found herself
alone. The much-debated French alliance had brought
definite gains. Up till now Florence's enemies had hesitated to press their molestation of her to the hilt. There
was nothing to stop them now. In August the League
decided to force Florence to change her government in
favour of the Medici—Cardinal Giovanni, his cousin
Giulio, his elder brother Giuliano, and his nephew
Lorenzo—and their army prepared to move into
Tuscany.

Florence continued to prepare herself for defence.

Machiavelli had spent most of the winter, after his return from Pisa, on military business, and this continued into the spring. On February 19th his light horse had their first full-scale parade in Florence, and on March 30th they were established by statute. This document, drawn up by Machiavelli himself, provided for five hundred horse 'to ensure liberty and the safety of the present government'. As with the infantry, the horse were only to be recruited in country districts; Florence was not so daunted by external threats that she was prepared to overlook internal ones. Throughout May and June Machiavelli was in and out of Florence, inspecting local garrisons and establishing strongpoints in the Val di Chiana. Everywhere there were enlistment figures to check, complaints to answer, inefficiencies to tidy up, and slack morale to tauten. A dispatch from the podestà of Montepulciano on June 27th shows him bringing comfort to this outpost. The town council was assembled and, 'as you may well imagine, Machiavelli exhorted them with great wisdom, and assured them, with most excellent and efficient reasons, that they had nothing to fear, either on this occasion or under more difficult circumstances, inasmuch as your Lordships had such an affection for them that you would never abandon them; to which he added other good words'. Much of this activity in the Val di Chiana was, in fact, wasted. Cardona, the League commander-in-chief, advanced from the direction of Bologna.

When August came, the month of invasion and defeat, Machiavelli was up in the Mugello, the invasion area. With so few men Florence could not hope to bar every possible route. The decision was taken, therefore, to concentrate troops at Firenzuola, half-way along one of the main routes from Bologna to Florence, and it is from Firenzuola that news of Machiavelli came on the 23rd in a dispatch from a commissary, Lamberto di Cambi. He and the mayor 'and Niccolò Machiavelli', he wrote, 'are in perfect harmony as to what is necessary to be done, and in providing for it. . . . If we could have had some three or four more gunners for the defence of this place we should have been very glad, but we are of good cheer and think ourselves quite safe. May it please our Lord God that it prove so in reality!' This was a vain hope. The army of the League had already outflanked Firenzuola by another route. On August 21st it appeared at Barberino.

The League's plans had been kept a close secret, and although the Florentines had sent an ambassador to a meeting of the confederates at Mantua, he had been pointedly snubbed and had gained no useful information. At first the Florentines were tempted to believe that there would be no invasion, that relations between the Spaniards and the Pope were too tense. Then they made the mistake of treating the approach of the League's army as a purely military threat, and making Firenzuola into an obstacle which no military expedition would like to have in its rear. But the League was calculating on revolution within Florence itself to supplement its military threat; its aim was to bring tension within the city to breaking-point by approaching quickly to within a few miles of its walls. So, without waiting to reduce Firenzuola, it passed round to Barberino, repeated a demand which Cardona had already made at the frontier that Florence should change her government and, when no answer was made, took Campi on the 27th. Buonaccorsi wrote that day to Machiavelli begging him on Soderini's behalf 'to take some action, because'—and the irony of the statement denotes a somewhat diminishing loyalty to the gonfalonier—the taking of Campi 'does not please him at all, and he is amazed at it'. He adds, 'Do what good you can, so that time is not lost in talk'.

Soderini's amazement was genuine. He had not been frightened by Cardona's swift advance. The city had readily granted money for the emergency, and though the League's army was composed of Spanish veterans, it was small, and Florence had a respectable force of some nine thousand men, of whom four thousand were in Prato, a centre which could not be lightly by-passed in a drive on Florence. Landucci noted on the 27th that peasants were streaming in from the country with panic in their hearts—'but their fear was not so great when they saw how the citizens were making preparations, and the poor creatures took heart, for in reality it seemed to intelligent people as if there were no need for fear; on the contrary, it was rather for the enemy to fear, because if they came down into these plains, they would fare badly. This was the opinion of every intelligent person. We had levied so many battalions of militia, and all the men-at-arms were eager to encounter the enemy'.

Next day the League army turned to Prato, strong-walled, well-garrisoned Prato. Cardona would have paused there to negotiate, but Machiavelli's efforts to seal the Mugello had been so successful that the army was short of supplies, and the order was given for an assault. The glamour of the prestige won by the militia as Pisa was speedily doused. The Spaniards had only two guns, and with these they made on the 29th a hole in the wall, 'which seemed', Nardi wrote, 'more like a window than a breach', because the masonry was still sound above it. Inside, right opposite the 'window' was the high wall of a monastery garden, and behind this again were pikemen and bowmen. But though they could easily have covered the breach, 'so great was the cowardice and sluggishness of the defenders', Nardi went on, 'that without any show of resistance they fled, scandalously throwing their arms to the ground, as though the enemy had suddenly been on their backs'. The horror of the subsequent sack filed the tongues with which writers later came to speak of the garrison, a good part of them conscripts and militia, and within a few weeks Machiavelli himself was to write of their 'cowardice', while Landucci's entry for the 29th expressed his amazement; these were four thousand defenders, 'and yet they all became as timid as mice and could not hold out for a single day'.

In spite of the fall of Prato, Florence itself remained, well garrisoned (as far as numbers were concerned) and with walls impregnable to a small army without a siege-train. But, as before, Cardona was not only relying on his military strength, he was anticipating Florence's political weakness. The Medicean party within the city was very strong. The Medici had made it clear that if they were to return it would be as mere private citizens. Events appeared to be favouring them : it was a good time to cross to the winning side. The cardinal had kept in touch with his sympathizers during the past weeks by means of letters carried in by a peasant and hidden in a wall of the cemetery of S. Maria

Novella,[1] and Giulio dei Medici had arranged a surreptitious meeting with Antonfrancesco degli Albizzi,
one of the Medicean party, at a villa outside the city.
On the 31st, while Cardona and his army remained
quietly at Prato, Albizzi and other Medicean supporters, including Paolo, Francesco Vettori's brother,
broke into the Palazzo della Signoria and called on
Soderini to resign. Soderini accepted the situation and
agreed, but sent Machiavelli to beg protection for him
from Francesco Vettori. This was granted, and the ex-
gonfalonier for life was escorted from the city, on the
way to exile on Turkish soil at Castelnuovo, near
Ragusa.

Soderini left on September 1st. Giuliano dei Medici
entered on the same day. Two days later an agreement
was signed with Cardona by which Florence agreed to
join the League and to permit the Medici to return as
private citizens. A new gonfalonier was elected, Gio-
vambattista Ridolfi, not for life, it is true : for fourteen
months, but otherwise it looked as though the Medici
had been peacefully absorbed into the existing constitution. Then, on September 16th, there was a carefully
stage-managed riot. The piazza della Signoria was suddenly aswarm with soldiers and citizens shouting *Palle!
Palle!* the Medici cry, while within the Palazzo della
Signoria Giuliano and others demanded a *parlamento*
in order to placate the mob and bring peace to the
city. Just as with Soderini a fortnight earlier, the government, reading the signs aright, did not bother to
protest too much. A *parlamento* was called, and the
people agreed to leave the introduction of changes in
the constitution to a *balìa*, or committee, of forty,

[1] I owe this detail to Miss Rosemary Hughes.

most of them Medici partisans. The acid of reform was splashed over the constitution of Savonarola : the Great Council was consumed, the militia and the Nine disappeared.

The Ten of War went, but Machiavelli had still the Second Chancery, and he was still its head. There is no record of his being used for any sort of business during the brief reign of Ridolfi, but as the new gonfalonier was a rival of Soderini's and an earnest devotee of Savonarola, this is hardly surprising. After the *coup d'état,* however, he wrote two documents designed to bring himself to the notice of the Medici. Reform of offices was very likely to be followed by a purge of officers, and though his chancery employment was secure (though subject to annual re-election) and his post still in existence, Machiavelli did not intend to wait for his reputation of being Soderini's *mannerino* to settle the future for him. Whatever his feelings about the Medici, he was not prepared to be quixotic, to follow his old leader into exile or resign in a fine republican rapture. Florence, after all, was still a republic, and though popular support had shrunk, and the government now expressed the wishes of one family, the future was still unsure; the immediate past had shown the dangers of weak leadership and division, and it was not yet clear that the Medici could surmount them. However, the Medici were now 'my masters', as he referred to them in a long letter [1] describing recent events, and he spoke of their return as providing some compensation for the dark days that culminated at Prato. To the cardinal he wrote a letter designed to help, but certainly not to flatter,

[1] To a woman whose identity is uncertain.

the Medici—suggesting, indeed, that they should change something they had already set in motion; they were arranging to get back their confiscated properties, and Machiavelli pointed out that less ill-feeling would be caused if the new owners were left in possession while the Medici were compensated by a money grant. He made this suggestion, he said, 'because men feel more grief at the loss of a farm than at the death of a father or brother'. He composed, too, an open letter of advice to the Medici[1] in which he warned them against those Florentines who denounced Soderini simply to curry favour with them. Again, this was advice but not fawning advice. He was clinging to the present but not denying the past. The tone of these communications is that of a servant of the state hoping to commend himself to the new régime through wisdom, not sycophancy.

The chancery was purged on November 7th. The First Chancellor, Marcello Virgilio, was left where he was; he had never meddled with politics or been identified with one particular party. But Machiavelli went, his place going to Niccolò Michelozzi, a Medicean. And Buonaccorsi went. Three days later came another blow. Machiavelli was condemned to remain in Florentine territory for a year, with a surety of one thousand gold florins. This move, which was presumably designed to cut him off from Soderini, was hard on account of the money rather than the limitation on his freedom of action, and it was followed on the 17th by an order forbidding him to enter the Palazzo della Signoria, though, as he was also made to justify the

[1] *Ai Palleschi.*

financial accounts of his period of office, this order had to be rescinded from time to time.

In the disillusion and distress caused by this treatment, Machiavelli received a letter from Soderini. It was written in such a way as to conceal the authorship as anyone detected in correspondence with the ex-gonfalonier would be suspected of treachery, and it contained a warning against any attempt at a reply. But Machiavelli was feeling too strongly to be cautious, and he wrote at length.[1] He answered the surprise Soderini expressed in his letter (which is lost) over the ease with which the transfer of power to the Medici took place. In families and in states, he said, the mood changes, and just as with a horse which is being ridden round and round a castle, one must change direction in order to keep it alert. Again, what would be the right action in one state would be wrong in another : the ruler must accommodate himself to circumstances ; this is why different methods applied in different states can, nevertheless, lead to the same result. In fact, the man whose aims are completely successful 'is the man who fits his course of action to the times'. There is, however, a difficulty ; man's nature is less flexible than the shifting pattern of events. If a man could not only see changes in the world about him but change himself, then he would succeed, and the saying that the wise man can rule the stars and the fates would be proved. But men are short-sighted, they cannot change their natures, and fate rules them instead. These, Machiavelli says, are basic problems, and just what is in-

---

[1] *Ghiribizzi scritti in Raugia al Soderini.* Best text in Mazzoni and Casella, *op. cit.*, pp. 878–880. We have only the rough copy, amended by Machiavelli.

volved in their solution 'I do not know—but I earnestly desire to know'.

Here, in replying to the bewilderment of Soderini, Machiavelli is attempting an answer to the sort of question which, in the vacancy of non-employment, he will be endlessly putting to himself. And in the same letter he uses what is to be a constant method of moving towards an answer. Reflecting on the fact that different means can bring about the same ends, he pointed out that Hannibal achieved by cruelty in Italy what Scipio achieved in Spain by moderation, and follows this with contemporary illustrations. 'Lorenzo dei Medici disarmed the people to retain Florence; Giovanni Bentivoglio armed them to hold Bologna. The Vitelli at Castello, and the present duke of Urbino in his dominions, dismantled their fortresses to hold their states; count Francesco [Sforza] and many others built them to secure theirs.' From things read and things seen he harks back to his main theme : the same problems sometimes call for different sorts of treatment; now it is the day of the legislator, now of the tyrant. A Hannibal would have failed in Spain; a Scipio would have failed in Italy. Without more ado, at this point the letter ends. The Scipio of the Florentine republic was being given, if not consolation, at least the explanation he had desired.

Later that winter, in mid-February, a piece of paper containing a list of names was accidentally dropped by a young man, Pietropaolo Boscoli, who was known to be an opponent of the Medici, in the house of a family related to the Soderini. It was brought to the notice of the government and a plot was suspected.

Boscoli and his closest associate, Agostino di Luca Capponi, were at once arrested, and confessed that they intended to change the government by assassination. They insisted that they had no party, had planned the *coup* alone, and that the names on the paper were simply those of men known to be friends of a free régime. The government, however, not surprisingly, followed them all up, and had them arrested on February 12th. One of them was Machiavelli.

As part of the interrogation which then took place, he was tortured by being given six hoists of the rope that bound his hands behind his back. He had nothing to confess, and the evidence against him and the other named friends of freedom was only suspicion, but they were held in the *Stinche*—the prison which had formerly been filled with Pisan prisoners. Boscoli and Capponi were executed while his own fate was still uncertain. Only on March 7th were the sentences on the others announced. Machiavelli was let off with a fine, and would be free when he had amassed the money— not an easy task, as he had already had to find a heavy security for his not leaving Florentine territory.

He felt no sense of involvement with Boscoli and Capponi, heroic young lovers of civic liberty though they were. He was merely the victim of a game they had played with names. In return for a slight acquaintance, they had brought him imprisonment, torture, and uncertainty. They had sent two of his close friends (also named on this list) away for two years' confinement in the ill-famed castle at Volterra. By clapping this scandal on his back they had considerably worsened his chances of getting employment under the Medici.

Machiavelli reacted by seeking to attract the attention of Giuliano—his most likely patron among the Medici—by disassociating himself from Boscoli and Capponi, and by presenting himself in the *persona* of a man of letters rather than that of a possibly controversial political figure. He wrote, not a formal petition, but a pair of sonnets, of which this is one :

> *Giuliano, I have jesses on my legs*
> *And six hoists of the rope across my back;*
> *I won't relate my other miseries,*
> *Because such torments poets never lack.*
>
> *About the walls creep lice as big as moths,*
> *Which in my dainty lodging-house have made*
> *A greater stench than there was ever known*
> *In Roncesvalles, or Sardinian glade.*
>
> *And there's a noise like the twin thundering*
> *Of Jove and Etna: lock and bolt and bar*
> *Clashing as one is chained, another freed,*
> *Another shrieks You're hoisting me too far!*
>
> *What pained me most was, as I slept towards dawn,*
> *Hearing the chanted prayers for the dead.*
> *Well, let them rot! so long as you, kind sir,*
> *Break my vile bonds, and pity me instead.*

He was released shortly after, not because of his poems but as the result of a general amnesty, for on March 11th Cardinal dei Medici was elected Pope as Leo X, in succession to Julius II who had died on February 20th. When this news reached Florence, bonfires began to blaze all over the city. The election showed that the Medici had come to stay; the rejoicing, that the populace was prepared to exchange the responsibilities of the Great Council for the prestige of a Florentine pope. It was more abundantly clear than ever that the only road to preferment lay through the Medici palace. For a month Machiavelli hung on in Florence, waiting for something to turn up. He was poor. The estate he had inherited from his father was cumbered with debts, and he had paid a share of it over to his brother Totto. He had a daughter and three sons to keep. He had tactfully written a 'Song of the Blessed Spirits' for the festivities which began with Leo's election, and he wrote another poem to Giuliano, a gay, off-hand jingle to accompany a gift of doves, but an open request for employment nonetheless. He had greater hopes of Francesco Vettori who, in spite of his services to the late government was in favour with the new one. Machiavelli had written on March 13th to announce his release from prison and to ask Vettori to put in a word on his behalf with the Medici, and he wrote again on the 18th, hoping that 'his masters' would find him something to do. 'And if nothing turns up, I must live as I did when I came into the world, for I was born poor, and learned to stint myself before learning to enjoy.' On March 30th Vettori reported that there was little to be expected from the new pope, but Machiavelli returned to his suit on April 16th. Guiliano had left for Rome : surely something could be found—if not at Florence, then at Rome, perhaps at the papal court itself.

Vettori was not the man to push an unwelcome suit. He was too self-regarding, and he was, besides, inhibited by the part he had played in protecting Soderini. He confessed in a letter of April 19th that he was not the right person to intervene on Machiavelli's

behalf. There was no one else who might help, so
Machiavelli retired from the expense and the associations of Florence to his house at Sant' Andrea in Per-
cussina, seven miles south of the city and two north
of S. Casciano, in the country.

CHAPTER SEVEN

The Setting of The Prince: *1513– 1514*

LIFE at Sant' Andrea had its own mild distractions. Machiavelli's house was beside the inn, and he owned a little woodland, some olives, and vines. He took pleasure in rural occupations, like bird-snaring, and in passing the afternoons in gossip and cards over a glass of wine, but these occupations could give pleasure only when part of a daily routine that was ballasted with something more weighty and absorbing. When in August he began to spend the evenings working at a treatise *De Principatibus*, they fell into place, but in the spring and early summer the burnt country-side must have seemed to him the *Stinche* where men were punished for being unemployed. From a career of often hectic industry, long journeys, and meetings with men whose levers moved the world, his horizon had shrunk to idleness and the chatter of a rural hamlet. Before leaving for S. Andrea he had told Vettori in a letter of April 9th that 'fortune has decreed that knowing nothing of silk manufacture nor the wool business, nor of profit or loss, I must talk politics, and unless I take a vow of silence I must discuss them'. And the politics he wished to talk was present politics. Dead politics, history, was to satisfy him later, as it had intrigued him before, but his instinct now was to discuss the political struggles of which he was himself a casualty—an instinct he determined to resist.

During the weeks after his release from prison there had been puzzling and threatening moves among the great powers. On March 23rd Louis had arranged a truce with Venice and on April 1st with Spain, which left him free to repair his fortunes in Italy. In Italy this gave rise to widespread bewilderment. Why had Ferdinand given his enemy a free hand? 'If this truce between France and Spain is true', Vettori wrote to Machiavelli on April 19th, 'either the Catholic King is not the astute and prudent man he is thought to be, or some mischief is brewing, and what has often been mooted has got into these princes' heads, and Spain, France, and the Emperor intend to divide up our poor Italy'. And returning to the subject two days later, he wrote : 'Since this truce is assured, I wish we could walk together from the Ponte Vecchio along via de' Bardi and on to Castello, and discuss what fancy has got into Spain's head.' And he ended : 'I would be glad of your opinion, because, to tell you the truth without flattery, I have found you to be sounder in these matters than any other man I have spoken to.'

This was an invitation that Machiavelli could not resist. It broke his resolve to forget current affairs and held him from finding solace in books. He replied from S. Andrea with a commentary on the political scene which ran to between two and three thousand words. 'While I read your letter', he wrote on April 29th, 'which I have read many times, I quite forgot my miserable state, and thought myself back in those activities which cost me—all for nothing—so much fatigue and time. And although I have sworn neither to think of nor discuss politics—my coming to stay in the country bears witness to that—all the same, to reply to your request, I am forced to break my vow.'

The next shift in the pattern of international relations was given by the battle of Novara on June 6th. Louis and the Venetians had attempted to take the Milanese from its duke, Massimiliano Sforza, but at this battle the French were completely routed by the Swiss, who, in their own interest, had constituted themselves the Duke's somewhat proprietory guardians. On June 20th Machiavelli gave his opinion in a letter dated from Florence, for he did not take his self-exile too literally, and escaped from time to time from the dullness of Sant' Andrea to the news, the women, and the drinking companions of the city. Though he was no longer concerned with political affairs, he said, he could not resist discussing them. Novara had been a great victory for the papal, anti-French party, and when Machiavelli referred to it as one of the events 'among the other great good fortunes, which have befallen his Holiness the Pope and that illustrious family', he was probably hoping that matters were more auspicious for his obtaining some favour from Leo, if Vettori should take up his suit again. He went on to survey the situation especially from Leo's point of view : what moves should the Pope take next ?

The correspondence continued through July and into August as a sort of political game. Each proposed a settlement that would bring peace to Italy and invited the other to criticize it. Their letters were full of reference to 'my peace' and 'your peace'. Machiavelli was prepared to make great concessions. France should have Milan and thus be satisfied ; Spain should have

Naples; the Pope the States of the Church; Venice should keep the bulk of her mainland possessions. The parties aggrieved by this arrangement would be the Duke of Milan (but he was an unimportant cipher) and Germany and the Swiss—but France would keep them in check. This 'peace' correspondence began from a suggestion from Vettori, but it was Machiavelli to whom it meant most. For Vettori it was largely a recreation, and, seeking a solution less passionately than Machiavelli, he was, in an off-hand way, less doctrinaire and more realistic, hoping less for a panacea than a stop-gap. For Machiavelli, with nothing else to do, the correspondence was a central preoccupation and, besides, there was always the hope that what he wrote would find its way to the eyes of the Medici.

In a letter of July 12th Vettori had said that Leo wanted to maintain the Church in all the possessions he found her endowed with 'unless to make over some to his relations Giuliano [his older brother] or Lorenzo [his nephew], to whom he is eager to give states'. It seemed that there would soon be new jobs for men of experience who could commend themselves to the Medici. Machiavelli did not represent himself as a man of glibly encouraging counsels. Vettori had seen Milan, Venice, and Ferrara as uniting to contain France and the Swiss. Machiavelli's answer was downright. Milan would always be a danger spot, with its weak duke and Swiss tutelege, he pointed out on August 10th. 'As for the union of the other Italians— you make me laugh. First, because there never will be any union that will do any good, and even if the leaders were united it would not be enough, for they have no arms worth a halfpenny. . . . In the second place, because the tails are not united to the heads—if this generation takes a step to further any cause, they fall to squabbling amongst themselves.' Vettori, on the 20th, attempted to defend the morale of Italian armies, pointing out that even the French were not uniformly effective. In 1494 they had promenaded through the peninsula, but Novara had seen them defeated, and now they were frightened by—of all countries—England, who had hardly known how to tell one end of a sword from another for twenty-five years.

Machiavelli replied on the 26th in a letter dated from Florence. The Italians, as at present organized in mercenary bands, would never change and become good soldiers. The best armies are those composed of native troops—it was so amongst the Romans and is true today of the Swiss. If the French could be victors one day and be vanquished another, can the Italians become victors in their turn? No. The French won against divided and mixed armies, and when they lost it was to national forces, like those of the Swiss (at Novara) and English (at the battle of the Spurs). He reviews the international situation, starting with a scathing description of the heads of states. Significantly, the only one who is flatteringly described is the Pope. 'We have a pope who is wise, prudent and respected; an unstable and fickle emperor, a haughty and timid king of France; a king of Spain who is miserly and close fisted; a king of England who is rich, wrathful and thirsty for glory; the Swiss—brutal, victorious, and insolent, and we Italians—poor, ambitious, and craven.' With this mixture any peace—either 'yours' or 'mine'—is difficult, and none likely. Nor can one be framed by reason alone. Monarchs behave so irrationally—as the Emperor with the Swiss, whom he should fear but does not—'that I hesitate to judge anything'. He confessed himself terrified by the situation. If France does not protect Italy (once given Lombardy, a condition of Machiavelli's 'peace') he sombrely concludes his letter, 'then I see no other remedy, and will now begin to mourn with you our ruin and slavery, which, if it does not happen today, or tomorrow, will come in our time'. This was the last letter he wrote to Vettori before telling him, on December 10th, that he had almost finished a short treatise *De principatibus*.

The Prince, as this work came to be known, is a natural outcome of Machiavelli's interest in external affairs, and in a sense is a continuation of the 'peace' correspondence in treatise form. He had not yet shown (as he was to show later in the *Discourses*) much interest in internal, constitutional affairs. His work for the Ten had led him to think primarily of Florence's impact on other states. He was concerned with Italian resistance to France and Spain, not with the balance of classes within his own city. He accepted the fact of Medicean domination. The Florentines had shown in their welcome of Giovanni and their rapture over his being made Pope that they endorsed the family's return. Machiavelli was still hopeful of employment. The Medici had as yet done nothing within Florence so threatening to the republican constitution as to divert his attention from the enthralling and tragic scenes in Italy and Europe as a whole. When he ceased to write to Vettori in August he continued to think about how to give strength to states which had no armies and little desire to unite against their common enemies. His diplomatic career had shown him some of the factors that led to power in the modern world, in Cesare Borgia he had seen an enthralling attempt to knock a new state together. Preoccupied with the need for drastic action in external affairs, it was natural for Machiavelli, though a republican in sympathy—was not the state which canalized the energies of all sections of the community potentially the strongest?—to think in terms of princes. To reason *de principatibus* was, besides, the most dynamic way of relieving his own nostalgia for action in diplomacy and war.

The work was a release, too, from personal distress. Writing to his nephew Giovanni Vernaccia on August 4th, Machiavelli tells him of the death of a three-day-old daughter, and says towards the end of the letter : 'I am well in body—but ill in every other way. And I see no hope save from God.' The letter of December 10th, perhaps the most famous letter ever written by an Italian, shows how the hours spent each day in his study helped to bring a measure of balance and even exhilaration into his life as a whole.

'I get up in the morning with the sun, and go into a wood of mine I am having cut down. I spend an hour or two there looking over the work done on the previous day and passing time with the woodcutters, who always have some quarrel on their hands, either among themselves or with their neighbours. . . . When I leave the wood I go to a spring and on from there with a book under my arm (Dante or Petrarch, or one of the minor poets like Tibullus, Ovid, or someone similar) to

an *uccellare* [1] which I have. I read of their amorous
passions and their loves; I remember my own—and for
a while these reflections make me happy. Then I move
on down the road to the inn, talk with passers-by, ask
news of the places they come from, hear this and that,
and note the various tastes and fancies of mankind.
This brings me to lunch-time, when I and my family
eat such food this poor house and my slender patrimony affords. When I have eaten, I go back to the inn,
where I usually find the landlord, a butcher, a miller,
and a couple of brick-makers. With these I act the
rustic for the rest of the day, playing at *cricca* and
tricche-trach, which lead to a thousand squabbles
and countless slanging matches—our fights are usually
over a farthing, but we can be heard shouting nonetheless from San Casciano. So, trapped among this vermin
I rub the mould off my wits and work off the sense of
being so cruelly treated by Fate—content to be driven
along this road if only to watch for her to show some
sign of shame.

'When evening comes, I return home and go into my
study. On the threshold I strip off the muddy, sweaty
clothes of everyday, and put on the robes of court and
palace, and in this graver dress I enter the antique
courts of the ancients where, being welcomed by them,
I taste the food that alone is mine, for which I was
born. And there I make bold to speak to them and
ask the motives of their actions. And they, in their
humanity, reply to me. And for the space of four hours
I forget the world, remember no vexation, fear poverty
no more, tremble no more at death : I am wholly
absorbed in them. And as Dante says that there can be
no understanding without the memory retaining what

[1] A spinney, usually on a hill-top, where nets were stretched
for snaring birds.

it has heard, I have written down what I have gained
from their conversation, and composed a small work
De principatibus, where I dive as deep as I can into
ideas about this subject, discussing the nature of
princely rule, what forms it takes, how these are
acquired, how they are maintained, why they are lost.
And if you have ever been pleased by any of my
fancies, this should not displease you. And it should be
acceptable to a prince, and especially to a new prince.
Therefore I am dedicating it to His Magnificance
Giuliano. Filippo Casavecchio has seen it; he can give
you details both of the work itself and the talk we have
had about it, though I am constantly plumping and
polishing it. . . .

'I have discussed this little work of mine with Filippo
as to whether I should give it to him [Giuliano] or
not, and whether, if I were to give it I should take it to
him myself or send it. Against presenting it there is
my suspicion that Giuliano would not read it, and
that Ardinghelli [1] would take the credit for this my
latest effort. For presenting it, there is the pressure of
my needs; I am becoming worn out, and I cannot
carry on like this for long without being harmed by
the stigma of poverty, and besides there is my longing that the Medici lords should begin to take me
into their service, even if they start by setting me to roll
stones, for if I could not then win them over, I should
have only myself to blame. As for this thing of mine, if
it were read it would be seen that I have not slept
through nor trifled with the fifteen years I have spent in
the study of statecraft, and anyone should be glad to
make use of a man who has gained so much experience
at other people's expense. And there need be no doubt
as to my good faith, for having always kept faith, I am

---

[1] One of the Pope's secretaries.

hardly going to learn how to break it now. One who has been, as I have, honest and faithful for forty three years is not likely to change his nature, and my poverty bears witness to my faith and honesty.

'So I would be grateful if you would write to tell me how the matter looks to you.'

At this important moment, then, the documents do not fail us. In the spring and summer the 'peace' correspondence showed his all-consuming interest in the international political scene. In the autumn, as this letter proves, he drew on his experience and his reading to add—though in a profoundly personal way—to the popular class of books *de regimine principum,* 'On Princely Rule'. And when it was drafted he began to see it as a possible means of getting employment and to think of dedicating it to the Pope's older brother, who was rumoured to be on the point of obtaining a principality of his own from the territories of the Church. How far *De principatibus* resembled the final *Il Principe* at this unplumped and unpolished stage is not known, but probably the only major change was the addition some time afterwards of the dedication and the last chapter, the exhortation to the dedicatee to liberate Italy from the barbarians.

The book was a discussion of princedoms, with special emphasis on new ones—the result of recent conquest, the products of change and themselves liable to change—and on how to render them stable through the exercise of special qualities by the prince himself, by his choice of agents and his use of a national army. Finally, Machiavelli justifies the book by showing that politics is a science from which men can learn, not just a learned recreation to be indulged in while Fortune dictates what is done; Fortune, he emphasizes, can, and must, be made to serve the deft and resolute prince. It was written to satisfy a need, but the impulse was a personal rather than a specific political one; the energy with which it was written imposed a unity of mood rather than of content. So far as is known, it was never subjected to final revision nor actually presented to Giuliano or his nephew Lorenzo, to whom Machiavelli dedicated it when Giuliano died in 1516.

The Prince reflects Machiavelli's fifteen years' experience in the chancery service. They had been years of war or of an uneasy peace that was scarcely distinct from war. The consistent good faith he vaunted in himself as an employee could be folly or treachery if practised by statesmen, under cover of whose purely pragmatic use of truth and falsehood ordinary citizens could indulge their own harmless rectitude. 'Everyone realizes how praiseworthy it is for a prince to honour his word and to be straightforward rather than crafty in his dealings; nonetheless contemporary experience shows that princes who have achieved great things have been those who have given their word lightly.' Machiavelli does not simply endorse the use of bad faith in case of necessity—the lie that diverts the killer from his victim—but as a natural part of statecraft. He had seen and admired the success of princes like Louis XII, Ferdinand, Cesare Borgia, Alexander VI and Julius II, and seen that all had depended at times on deception. As an amateur of war he was familiar with the need for stratagem and deceit, and had read the praise of these devices in ancient writers on military matters. As a diplomatist he had combated men who were professionally committed to outwit and deceive him; as Soderini's *mannerino* he had been the victim of malice and intrigue. He had, besides, a relish for cleverness, whatever form it took. All these factors, together with the dramatic form in which he couched his arguments, help to push his observations on good faith and bad faith to an extreme. If men were good, then one should be good in return, 'but because men are wretched creatures, who would not keep their word to you, you need not keep your word to them.' Machiavelli could not observe without exhorting. It is the 'go thou and do likewise' tone that has caused offence, not the evidence from which this advice is deduced. His impatience of observation for its own sake, without it being stripped, as it were, for action, led him to omit saving clauses which might otherwise humanize his statements. 'Men will always be false to you unless they are compelled by necessity to be true' is not a statement to be literally maintained by a man in the circle of his family and friends, but in the form 'A statesman in time of crisis should act as though men will always be false', it is less open to criticism. Moreover, his assumption that craft and cruelty are necessary is accompanied by an acceptance that they stain a prince's noblest attribute—his glory.

There is hardly a year from Machiavelli's career in the chancery that cannot be shown to have provided some evidence, or reflection on events, that helped to shape *The Prince*. A clear reference to his French experience that justice and reason are but subsidiary weapons—that the unarmed man is 'Ser Nihilo'—is to be found in Chapter 14, which is about the need for a national army. 'Among other evils caused by being disarmed, it renders you contemptible.' *The Prince* contains three chapters on soldiers. The worst sort are mercenary—and he instances Vitelli. Only slightly better are friendlies, auxiliaries —and he describes the perils that threatened Florence owing to her use of French troops against Pisa. Then, 'I shall never hesitate to cite Cesare Borgia and his conduct as an example', Machiavelli wrote, and went on to describe how, after experimenting with mercenary and auxiliary troops, Cesare came to rely upon his own subjects. The lessons of the mission to Cesare and the advice of the tract *Remarks on the raising of money* recur here in extended form : negotiation must be based on strength; neutrality is fatal. And the warning he gives there that the Florentines have a baneful optimism which sees a day's sunshine as lasting for ever is echoed in a warning to princes not to be taken unawares by war 'as it is a common fault of men not to reckon on storms during fair weather'. The judicial murder of Ramiro Lorqua, brusquely reported in the dispatch of December 26th, 1502, now becomes a symbol of wisely resolute political action. In Chapter 12 when Machiavelli states that 'the main foundations of every state, new states as well as ancient or composite ones, are good laws and good arms', we hear an echo from the infantry ordinance, and his reflections in Chapter 6 on the problems facing a reformer, whose own side only supports him half-heartedly while his opponents fight *à l'outrance,* reflect his own teething troubles with the militia. The chapter 'How much human affairs are governed by fortune, and how fortune may be opposed' is almost all extended from passages in the letter to Soderini in Ragusa ; so, too, the musing on the phenomenon of different means pro-

ducing identical ends, the conclusion that 'the successful man is he whose mode of procedure accords with
the needs of the times.' In chapter 3 of *The Prince,*
about states that absorb new territories, the tone of the
argument—concise, intense, and personal—and the
matter itself (the problem is illustrated by the recent
behaviour of the French in Italy) make it seem like a
continuation of the 'peace' correspondence. This
chapter epitomizes the way in which Machiavelli
called on his past experience. The point that 'men
must be either pampered or crushed' was made in
1503 in the pamphlet on the Val di Chiana rebellion.
His scorn of those who play for time instead of taking
active precautions was confirmed, as we have seen, by
his earliest diplomatic encounters. He goes on to
elaborate the argument he had had with d'Amboise in
1500 about the errors of French policy in Italy.
D'Amboise had defended French support of the Borgia
by referring to promises made by Louis to Alexander
VI. Machiavelli's comment in *The Prince* is fortified
by the behaviour of Julius II in cancelling papal
promises to the Bolognese. 'A prudent ruler', he says,
'cannot, and should not, honour his word when it
places him at a disadvantage, and when the reasons
for which he made his promise no longer exist.'

This dour conclusion was the result of his own observation, and this is true of all the conclusions in *The
Prince.* Conversations with the illustrious shades of
antiquity play a much smaller part than the letter of
December 10th might have led Vettori to believe, and
he illustrates all his important points by quoting contemporary instances. He repeats his double indebtedness in the dedication. 'I have not found among my

belongings anything as dear to me or that I value as much as my understanding of the deeds of great men, won for me from a long acquaintance with contemporary affairs and a continual study of the ancient world.' But this statement, though it increased the fashionableness and respectability of the work, conceals the dependence on raw contemporary experience.

His use of historical illustrations was rhetorical and arbitrary. In the last years of his life, when writing the *History of Florence*, he arranged his evidence, and sometimes warped it, to drive home general principles. He does this even more in the earlier work, where he was not concerned with the past, even the immediate past, as such. He cuts the film to obtain significant stills. Cesare Borgia's shoddy decline becomes irrelevant; 'I know of no better precepts to give a new prince than ones derived from Cesare's actions,' he writes in Chapter 7. He is not concerned to re-create. His aim is to expose in history the nerve of resolute actions. He is not concerned to qualify his conclusions. The hesitations, the exceptions, the safeguards could be shaded in when they were applied to particular situations. When he comes to a subject which cannot be reduced to black and white, he moves aside. 'There are many ways in which a prince can win [the people] over. These vary according to circumstances, so no definite rule can be given and I shall not deal with them here.' The style he uses shows a similar scorn of sinuosities. There are few literary flowers: a handful of metaphors and analogies, most of these being pithy, familiar, and racy, and one parable in which David is shown refusing Saul's arms when he goes out against Goliath: 'arms belonging to someone else either fall from your back [mercenaries], or weigh you down [auxiliaries], or impede your movements [a mixture of both].'

Machiavelli was not seeking in *The Prince* to give specific advice for the present situation, but the book is vibrant, nevertheless, with the conviction that advice is needed and that he is the one to give it. 'The wish to acquire more', he remarks in Chapter 3, 'is admittedly a very natural and common thing.' It followed that change and flux should be taken as a norm, and that rulers should never relax their vigilance. There was a danger, especially when disasters were coming thick and fast, that men would throw up their hands and declare themselves the playthings, not the masters, of events. The book stresses man's responsibility to act; fortune—the pattern of events—can be directed by the self-reliant man. It is true that, in one sense, Cesare's own downfall 'was not his fault but arose from the extraordinary and inordinate malice of fortune', but in another sense he fell because, at a moment of crisis, he wavered; though ill at the time of Pius III's election, on that pope's death he should not have supported Giuliano della Rovere, who, as Julius II, remembered all too clearly the injuries that Cesare had formerly done him. 'So the duke's choice was a mistaken one, and it was the cause of his ultimate ruin.' Men should never blame fate for their disasters; 'the only sound, sure, and durable methods of defence are those based on your own actions and prowess.'

The importance of his work, and its novelty, Machiavelli claimed, resided in the fact that he was concerned only with *il vero*, the true picture of what actually happened, and that he only talked about politics in terms directly deduced from the way in which men had behaved and did behave. To have a private morality up one's sleeve and put it to one's nose when the stench of political morality became too great was sheer hypocrisy. Referring to the extreme cruelty of Hannibal, he noted that 'the historians, having given little thought to this, on the one hand admire what Hannibal achieved, and on the other condemn what made his achievements possible.' But you cannot have it both ways—admire the end and deplore the means. Machiavelli emphasized that his approach (familiar enough in discussion and dispatch) was something new in a work of political theory. Writing for statesmen, he will do them the service of writing in terms that they can apply directly to the problems of the real world. 'Since my intention is to say something that will prove of practical use to the enquirer', he emphasized in Chapter 15, 'I have thought it proper to represent things as they are in real truth, rather than as they are imagined . . . the gulf between how one should live and how one does live is so wide that a man who neglects what is actually done for what should be done learns the way to self-destruction rather than self-preservation. The fact is that a man who wants to act virtuously in every way necessarily comes to grief among so many who are not virtuous. . . . If a person wants to maintain his rule he must learn how not to be virtuous, and to make use of this or not according to need.' Quixotry, in fact, is one of the worst foibles a statesman can indulge in.

There was naturally an embarrassment in talking so frankly even in a manuscript not intended, so far as

we know, for the press, but this <u>insistence on a double</u>
<u>standard of morality, a sense of private right and wrong</u>
<u>from which the responsible ruler must diverge as neces-</u>
<u>sity dictates, is made to play a surprisingly emphatic</u>
<u>role in *The Prince*</u>. One more example will suffice to
show how Machiavelli laboured the point. 'You have
to understand this, that a prince, and especially a new
prince,' he wrote in Chapter 18, 'cannot observe all
those things which give men a reputation for virtue, because, in order to maintain his state, he is often compelled to act in defiance of good faith, of charity, of
human courtesy, of religion.' The point about this
remark is not that it is shocking but that it is obvious.
The lessons of *The Prince* do not require the anxious
moral glosses with which Machiavelli surrounds them.
Statesmen had been functioning efficiently on Machiavellian lines for centuries, and by begging them to be
self-conscious about the motives for their actions,
Machiavelli was not aiding but embarrassing their
freedom of action.

If Macchiavelli had been born to the ruling class,
he would not have been concerned to defend its acceptance of expediency. As it was, he could not identify
himself with the prince without bringing with him the
conscience of a subject. For all its dogmatic force there
is a tentative, apologetic note in *The Prince*. This is
what I would do, Machiavelli seems to be saying, and
this is why it would be allowable for me to do it. The
streak of republican high-mindedness, which was never
far beneath the surface in Florence, forced Machiavelli
to make those explanations which blackened his reputation with posterity. There were complex motives
which helped him identify himself with the interests of

his Prince : confidence in his own powers, frustration at the bungling of others, a sense of urgency, the glamour of power; but none of these lifted him clear of the standards of his family and his class. Princes, especially new princes, must use cruelty and fraud to secure themselves, he wrote, and princes all over Europe would have greeted this dictum with an acquiescent and unalarmed nod. But Machiavelli could not leave the matter there. He elaborated, saying of cruelties : 'We can say that cruelty is used well (if it is permissible to talk in this way of what is evil) when it is employed once for all, and one's safety depends on it, and then it is not persisted in.' It is as though Machiavelli's prince had started life as an honest bourgeois, and needed constant reassurance that he need act no longer as a private citizen. The assumption that political action would be based on expediency was part of Machiavelli's novel approach to his subject; the labouring of this assumption a reminder that he brought to it a not altogether unconventional state of mind.

Machiavelli had to wait until December 24th before receiving a reply to his letter of the 10th, and then Vettori only referred to the news about *De principatibus* in a sidelong way, saying that he could not see any suitable opening for Machiavelli in Rome, but would think more seriously about it when he had seen the manuscript. And when he had received part of it, he merely said (on January 18th, 1514) that he was exceedingly pleased with the work but would not commit himself until he had seen the whole. It is not, perhaps, surprising that Vettori was so reticent. If he had openly admired *The Prince*, he could hardly have avoided pressing Machiavelli's claims to a post with the Medici, and this was the sort of morally courageous effort he shrank from. Machiavelli's disappointment was probably tempered by resignation. He knew that Vettori was not the man to push hard for a friend's advantage, and there is no hint of resentment in his next letters. The book had been written, moreover, primarily for its own sake, not for use as a testimonial.

Vettori, though he ignored *The Prince*, repeated to its author an invitation to come to Rome which he had already made in the previous November. Machiavelli again hesitated. There would be embarrassment in meeting old acquaintances, like Cardinal Soderini, in new circumstances. He had no hope that proximity to the Vatican would help his chances of employment there. And it would involve expense which he could ill afford. He had to write to Vettori on April 16th to beg him to intervene on his behalf over unpaid taxes, and Vettori wrote to the officials concerned to bear witness that Machiavelli was, in fact, incapable of paying them. In spite of this relief, Machiavelli wrote on June 10th in a mood of deep despondency: 'If God does not treat me better I shall have to leave home one of these days and take a job as a constable's book-keeper or secretary if I can find nothing else, or bury myself as a schoolmaster in some out-of-the-way spot in the country, and leave my family here—they would be as well off if I were dead . . . I am not writing this to get you to put yourself out for me in any way, but simply to get it out of my system, and so that I shall not have to write any more on such an odious theme.'

The greater part of their correspondence in 1514, however, was of a frivolous nature, with Vettori setting the tone. Vettori was gregarious, yet liable to fits of melancholy; he shrank from crowded court life and ambassadorial pomps on the one hand and intimacy on the other. In the Roman *demi-monde* and in correspondence with Machiavelli he found a congenial mean. They wrote much about mutual friends, like the innkeeper Donato del Corno, well-to-do, bonhomous, and fairly influential—he had made, and was trying to get back, loans to the present government—and about Vettori's love affairs. Commenting on one of these in a letter of February 4th, Machiavelli ruefully describes himself as getting on everyone's nerves, whether it is in Donato's tavern or at another favourite rendezvous, the house of a courtesan called La Riccia, but he can at least throw himself into Vettori's concerns. 'And since my own case makes you uneasy, remembering what I have suffered from the arrows of Love, I must tell you how I behave with him now: in fact, then, I let him have his way, and follow him through vales and woods, cliffs and fields, and found that he has granted me more favours than if I had treated him roughly. Throw off the heavy saddle, then; take out the bit; shut your eyes and say: "Do what you will, Love; lead me, guide me; if I have good fortune I will sing your praises, if ill, the fault will be yours; I am your slave".' And he added: 'If you want a serenade for her, I offer to come with some fine conceit that will fill her with love.'

On February 25th he wrote to Vettori about two of their mutual friends, both loose-living, one preferring boys, the other women. The former, Giuliano Brancacci tracks down a boy one dark night in Florence, seduces him and then says: 'I've no money on me. But my name is Filippo di Casavecchia; come and ask me for the money tomorrow morning.' The consequences of this episode are worked up into what amounts to something like a full-blown *novella*. After telling the story Machiavelli ended: 'To your last letter I have nothing to answer except—follow love *totis habenis*, and the pleasure you take today, you will not have to seek tomorrow, and if things are still as you describe them, I envy you more than the king of England. I beg you follow your star, and do not care a jot for the things of this world, because I believed, believe, and always will believe that Boccaccio's saying is a true one: that it is better to act and to repent, than to do nothing and repent.'

These letters, in which the pleasure of the moment is urged to the lover with as much energy as the pursuit of power had been to the ruler, followed the realization that Vettori was not greatly interested in *The Prince*. They were written from Florence. By May or June he was back at the farm, probably to save money, and it was from the farm that he followed his gloomy letter about going off to be a constable's secretary with one that defiantly turned its back on 'this most odious of all possible themes'. At last he has a romance of his own to rival Vettori's, 'for, being back in the country', he wrote on August 3rd, 'I have met a creature so charming, so delicate', etc., that he cannot do her justice. Just as Vettori had described the first stirrings of *his* love, so will Machiavelli, 'understand, then, that they were nets of gold, laid among flowers, woven by Venus, so soft and mild that though an insensitive heart might have broken through them I did not want to'. He emphasized that this was an affair of no ordinary significance, and that though 'nearly in my fiftieth year, this does not trouble me, nor do rough ways tire me, nor the darkness of the nights dismay me'. Machiavelli was only forty-five when he wrote this, and we must not imagine him struggling towards his rustic love along actual rough paths through palpable darkness; these are literary fancies, as we know from his use of them in the letter of February 4th. Some actual affair might have provided the motive for this romantic fantasy just as it might have provided the motive for the sordid one in his letter to Luigi Guicciardini, but this letter does little more than show his anxiety and frustration—for he was still not resigned to non-employment by the Medici—venting themselves in another form of escapism. 'I have renounced thoughts of grand and weighty things,' he went on. 'It no longer charms me to read of the ancient world, nor to discuss the contemporary one. . . . If you want to write anything about your love, do so, and discuss other things with those who value them more, and understand them better, because they have brought me nothing but loss.'

Towards the end of the year, however, Vettori brought him back to politics. He wrote on December the third to propose that they should resume their discussion of the international situation, and especially that Machiavelli should image what measures would best strengthen the dominion of Leo X. He was to suppose that the Pope wanted to maintain the prestige of the Church, but found himself faced by a situation in which France, with Venetian aid, was determined to take Milan, while the Emperor, with Ferdinand and the Swiss, were determined to defend it. What should

the Pope do : aid France? aid the others? or remain
neutral? And Vettori went on to say, 'I would like you
to give me your opinion on this in such a way as you
imagine that your letter were to be seen by the Pope.
. . . I promise to show it, as your work, when I judge
the moment ripe.' And he ended, rather formally, as
though he had been directed to write on these lines,
'though you have been away from your office for two
years, I do not believe that you have forgotten its art.'

Machiavelli replied with a long letter on December
10th, and he followed this up on the 20th with two
more, one continuing the discussion, the other suggesting that the time might be ripe for raising the question
of employment again. The first letter was written with
a return to his most energetically donnish style. 'If a
prince wishes to know which of two combattants will
win, he must first measure the resources and the morale
of one and the other.' Machiavelli's conclusion was
that Leo should support France, and it was argued
with the use of the dominant 'peace' correspondence
themes. The second letter was hardly more than an
essay on the dangers of neutrality. The third made an
open statement of his longing for employment by the
Medici, in Florence or outside it.

Vettori's answer to these letters was discouraging.
Writing from Rome on December 30th he said that
he had shown them to the Pope, and both he and the
Cardinal dei Medici had praised them highly—but,
he warned, no defin'te offer was made, in part, perhaps, because 'I am not one of those men who know
how to help their friends'. It was little comfort that he
added at the end : 'I am not one of those who fill their
friends with vain hopes.' Having to rely on Vettori as

his closest friend was no way to improve Machiavelli's faith in mankind as a whole.

When he replied, however, on January 31st, 1515, there was no change in his tone; the letter, indeed, summed up quite consciously the nature of their correspondence as a whole. It was in two parts; the first was about his delicious slavery to love, the second was about politics, and the two parts were joined by the following bridge passage. 'Anyone who was to see our letters, my dear friend, and saw how diverse they were, would be much amazed, because it would seem to him that now we were grave persons, absorbed in weighty matters, and that no thought could leave our minds that was not virtuous and lofty, and then, turning the leaf, he would find the same men frivolous, fickle, lecherous and interested only in trifles. Now this way of going on may seem blameworthy to some, but to me it seems worthy of praise: we model ourselves on nature, who herself is various, and one cannot be blamed for imitating her. And although we usually show this variety in separate letters, I wish to show it this time in one, as you will see if you read the other side. So rinse out your mouth.'

The other side was given up to speculation about a visit paid recently to Florence by Giuliano dei Medici and his majordomo, Vettori's brother Paolo. Machiavelli had heard that there were plans to make Giuliano lord of a state consisting of Parma, Piacenza, Modena, and Reggio. Commenting that this was a fine plan but a difficult one to implement, Machiavelli wrote, 'in maintaining these new states, ruled by a new lord, endless problems are involved'—especially when, as in this case, there was no natural unity between the parts.

'Duke Valentino, whose proceedings I would always imitate if I were a new prince' had used Ramiro Lorqua as his agent and owed much of his success in the Romagna to him. Giuliano, then, should chose Paolo as his lieutenant. Machiavelli added that he had put this idea to Paolo, who had been pleased by it.

It is possible that it was at this point that Machiavelli took up *The Prince* and on rereading it gained the impetus to crown it with the 'Exhortation to Liberate Italy from the Barbarians'. Here at last, through Paolo's patronage, was the longed-for chance of employment with the Medici. Here was a concrete proposal which would call for talents such as his, and a situation to which much of the subject-matter of *The Prince* was directly relevant. Italy now stood in even greater peril of invasion than at the end of 1513. He began by dwelling on the urgency of the situation. In his letter of December 10th, 1514, he had urged a French alliance; now, in this last chapter, with an optimism of which there had been no trace in his correspondence in 1513, he urged that the opposing Swiss and Spanish armies were not invincible. He referred again, as he had in the recent letter of January 31st, to Duke Valentino—'a gleam of hope has appeared before now which gave hope that some individual might be appointed by God for her redemption, yet at the highest summit of his career he was thrown aside by fortune.' Now there was a second chance to save Italy. But salvation must come from strength—and Machiavelli, the creator of the militia, and identified with it as with no other aspect of his career, spent more than a third of his space stressing the need for an indigenous army trained on lines superior to the recently reconstituted militia forces, damaging the literary shape of the chapter for the sake of an emphasis that would direct attention to his own qualifications for employment.

This personal plea, and the note of passionate faith that Italy's salvation could be at hand which occurs in two paragraphs of this exhortation, were vain. Cardinal dei Medici, who had known of Machiavelli's ideas through Francesco Vettori, had not been softened by them. On hearing of Paolo's interest in Machiavelli he wrote to Giuliano to forbid his employment. Once more Machiavelli had to turn from thoughts of an active life to one of reflection; from an absorption with external relations and the actions of princes to a growing concern with internal relations and constitutional expedients. He was not to write to Vettori again for twelve years. Modern events had no place for him. He turned instead to the study of the past.

CHAPTER EIGHT

The Oricellari Gardens. The Discourses and Literary Works: 1515–1519

DURING the six years from 1515 to 1520, Machiavelli wrote the greater part, some two-thirds, of his literary works, the *Discourses*,[1] *The Golden Ass*, the *Dialogue on our Language*, *Mandragola*, *The Art of War*, and *The Life of Castruccio Castracani*. He also produced other poems beside *The Golden Ass*, and it was probably during this period that he wrote his short story, *Belfagor*. It was a period of international tension, but not, from the autumn of 1515, of open war. In September the French defeated the Swiss defenders of Lombardy at Marignano and occupied Milan and Genoa. Leo came to an agreement with the new French king, Francis I, whereby in return for ceding Parma and Piacenza the Pope was allowed a free hand throughout the rest of the Papal States. He took advantage of this in May of the next year when Lorenzo dei Medici expelled Duke Francesco Maria della Rovere from Urbino and was appointed Gonfalonier of

[1] This accepts the thesis that the *Discourses* were not begun in 1513, as an older generation of Machiavelli students accepted —and, it should be noted, still assert (Ridolfi, *op. cit.* in bibliography p. 480; Chabod, *op. cit.* pp. 31–2). It was first suggested by Hans Baron in *Bibliothèque d'Humanisme et Renaissance*, 1956, after a reconstruction of the genesis of the *Discourses* by Felix Gilbert in the *Journal of the History of Ideas*, 1953. Dr. Baron has convincingly elaborated his views in an article he was kind enough to show me, and which is to appear in 1961 in the *English Historical Review*.

the Church. In 1517 Francesco Maria took back his duchy, only to lose it again a few months later when he finally surrendered to the Pope. These changes of fortune at Urbino were the only breaches of the peace within Italy during those years.

Machiavelli was able to indulge his intellectual interests without having his attention drawn imperatively outside the bounds of Florence. Only once did the wars of Urbino break into his privacy. Giuliano had died on March 17th, 1516, leaving *The Prince* without a dedicatee. In the same month his nephew Lorenzo, aged twenty-one, as captain-general of the Florentines led the papal armies against Urbino and successfully occupied the duchy. He was a much discussed figure, the most likely gatherer-up of Italian fragments since Cesare Borgia. A Venetian ambassador, Mario Giorgi, described him as 'of a bold temperament, shrewd, fitted for great deeds, and if not equal to Valentinois, very little behind him'. Machiavelli substituted his name for that of Giuliano, though it is not known if he actually presented him with *The Prince*. There is a story to the effect that he did, but that Lorenzo was more interested in a pair of greyhounds which were presented to him at the same time. It is not, basically, an unlikely tale. Lorenzo was already a new prince and scarcely needed to study how to become one; he was the most active member of his family, and, as Machiavelli recognized in Chapter 23 of *The Prince*, the ruler most capable of putting advice into effect is least likely to ask for it. Even without the additional factor of Machiavelli's name being on the Medici black-list, there was a presumption that Lorenzo would prefer the greyhounds.

Machiavelli's revived hopes for *The Prince* must have come to a head between Giuliano's death and the following October, when Lorenzo was made duke of Urbino, but apart from this flutter of ambition, Machiavelli was left free to make the most of a leisure which lost some of its bitterness as he came to see more and more of a new circle of associates, liberal *ottimati* and their literary friends, men who compensated for the Medici's failure to offer employment by offering, besides some practical patronage, open admiration and encouragement. They met as an informal discussion group in the Oricellari gardens. Bernardo Rucellai, who had laid them out in the previous century, had been a close friend of the Medici, rich, cultivated, a man of letters himself with a wide acquaintance attracted by his hospitality and the breadth of his interests. He had been a patron of the arts second, perhaps, only to Lorenzo himself, and as long as Lorenzo lived had been near the centre of political affairs. He had crossed swords with Piero, however, and after 1494 held a somewhat enigmatic position, a republican by sympathy but unable to approve of the radical cast given to the constitution by Savonarola. He approved the creation of the life gonfaloniership, but rapidly came to dislike Soderini, eventually leaving Florence and making no secret of the fact that, while not actually intriguing treacherously with the Medici, he would welcome the overthrow of Soderini and of the Great Council.

Before his absence and after his return in 1512, the gardens were a rendezvous for friends interested in literary and political topics. Fashionable subjects like the rival claims of Latin or the vernacular were de-

bated there, the political institutions of the Romans
were discussed, and the relevance of the Venetian
model of government to the problems of Florence. It
was an environment in which Machiavelli's own interests, in fact, found a congenial welcome. It was,
moreover, a place of great charm. Rucellai had super-
intended the design of the garden with great care. It
was between the inner and outer circuits of the walls,
looking up to Fiesole. There was a summer-house, and
beside the paths were marble benches and busts of
great figures from the Roman past, statesmen and men
of letters. The beds were full of rare flowers, for it had
been Rucellai's fancy to collect as many as he could of
the flowers mentioned in classical literature. In spite of
a tendency to idealize the wise, firm days of Lorenzo,
the atmosphere was by means one of cultural nostalgia; there was sympathy for novelty as well. Rucellai's
son Giovanni wrote the first tragedy in the vernacular,
Rosmunda, and Bernardo wrote in his *De bello Gallico*
the first attempt to assess the consequences of Charles
VIII's invasion as well as to describe its cause.

Bernardo died in 1514, but meetings continued
under the charming and cultivated Cosimino Rucellai.
'This Cosimino', wrote Iacopo Nardi, himself a member of the Rucellai group, 'by ill chance was infected
by syphilis in early adolescence, and after treatment
remained crippled, so that he was bound to an invalid's
couch, or rather to a light bed which could be easily
moved from place to place. . . . It was for Cosimino
and the other members that Machiavelli had written
and dedicated his *Discourses,* a work which certainly
dealt with a novel topic, never attempted before, so
far as I know, by anyone else. For this Niccolò was

thought of very warmly by them, and they gave him, I know, some financial assistance. They greatly relished his conversation, and valued all his work very highly.' The extent of Machiavelli's absorption in this circle and his indebtedness was seen in other works besides the *Discourses*, which were dedicated to Cosimino Rucellai and Zanobi Buondelmonti. These two men appear among the *dramatis personæ* of the later *Art of War*, along with Battista della Palla and Luigi Alamanni, also frequenters of the gardens. When *Castruccio Castacani* was finished, Machiavelli sent it to Buondelmonti and Alamanni for their opinions. Among other visitors were the poet Iacopo da Diacceto, and the historians Iacopo Nardi and Filippo Nerli. The company of the gardens provided a challenge to Machiavelli's strongest interests and a sympathetic audience for them.

During 1516 and 1517, then, stimulated by members of Rucellai's circle, he carried his commentary on the first ten books of Livy's *History of Rome* into the form which we know as the *Discourses*. It is not known precisely in what way the book progressed. When Machiavelli was first invited to the gardens, he may already have begun making notes on Livy with a systematic treatise in mind; he may have read some sections in the gardens or, more likely, to have introduced as topics for discussion, matters which he later worked up into chapters for the *Discourses*. There is no reason to doubt that Rucellai and his companions became increasingly involved in the progress of the work. It suited their mood well enough with its acknowledgment of the greatness of Rome and its search for working solutions to contemporary problems, and Machiavelli's preoccupation with republics was no embarrassment to a circle which included members of the Medicean party : that family always protested its intention to remain private citizens and did not see its interests as discordant with the prevailing admiration for republican Rome. At no stage in his life did Machiavelli show himself to be in the class of revolutionary, or even particularly urgent, republicans, and in a chapter 'Of Conspiracies' in the *Discourses* Machiavelli quotes approvingly, 'a golden sentence of Cornelius Tacitus, where he says "that men should honour the past and obey the present ; and whilst they should desire good princes, they should bear with those they have, such as they are"—and surely', he adds, 'whoever acts otherwise will generally involve himself and his country in ruin'.

In the dedication Machiavelli harped on his practical experience of politics in almost the same words that he used in the dedication of *The Prince* : 'I have endeavoured to embody in it all that long experience and assiduous reading have taught me of the affairs of the world.' As with *The Prince,* certain passages elaborated ideas that had arisen from his work for the Ten, and had already been expressed in occasional writings, like his memorandum on the rebels of the Val di Chiana or in letters, especially those written to Soderini and Vettori after his dismissal. The *Discourses*, like *The Prince*, were never revised for the press, they were not printed in Machiavelli's lifetime, and it is hazardous to conjecture from the work as it stands what its final form would have been.

It remains, as a result, a personal document, a seriatim record of how Machiavelli thought about miscellaneous political issues, rather than a corpus of measured conclusions. Machiavelli never wrote a credo. He never put his hand on his heart and said, 'I believe . . .' It is doubtful, in fact, if he had a coherent set of conclusions to offer. He identified himself readily with the protagonists of his reading and experience, whether prince, general, prophet, or patriotic republican. His random reflections on politics were not systematized by a firm sense of social caste, as were those of Guicciardini, who saw the responsible exercise of power by the *ottimati* as the essential nucleus of any constitutional theory, and they were not kept in bonds by some dominating theory, theocentric or contractual. Machiavelli's political ideas are incapable of summary. His writings abound in contradictions, and in hares that have been started and not run to ground. He was not a systematizer but a commentator, and the *Discourses*, as a deliberate commentary, was his most characteristic work. As he reads through Livy, associations from books or his own career come now in a flood, now sparsely, and he accepts the flow without seeking to adjust it to a uniform pressure. Some chapters are long essays which needed no passage from Livy to justify them, others are hardly more than brief notes on the text. His fascination with the problems involved in action blind him to the obviousness of some of his generalizations—as when he asserts that 'Nothing is more worthy of the attention of a good commander than to endeavour to penetrate the designs of the enemy'. Sometimes a chapter heading reveals that he has exploited one of the popular debating topics of the day : 'Whether an able commander with a feeble army, or a good army with an incapable commander, is more to be relied on.'

Such 'message' as there was can be stated baldly as follows :

'A Republican constitution is best for Florence. At present the citizens are not strong willed enough to sustain the responsibilities of self-government and the perils of war. The body-politic must be disciplined by a sound military organization and by a religious teaching that emphasizes the active rather than the contemplative side of the faith. Regeneration can be best organized by a prince, but when he feels that civic virtue has been restored, he should retire. The leaders of all states whether princely or republican, should learn from history how to behave in the contemporary world.'

The return of the Medici power to a Florence whose citizens had shown themselves 'corrupt' before 1512 provided a background of verisimilitude to this general statement ; Machiavelli probably used the term 'prince' to include the Medici resident in Florence plus the support of Leo from Rome.

While the form of the *Discourses* is loosely that of a commentary, its tone is exhortatory. He constantly uses phrases like 'this example should be followed— imitated—adopted—observed.' He is not using his comments on Livy to explain the *History of Rome* but to point his observations on actual affairs or political theory. His didactic intention is made clear in the Introduction to Book Two ; in bad times like the present, men must learn from times that were more healthy and imitate the men of those days. His own role, in his retirement, is to explain the lessons.

The key to his approach is his conviction that man can learn from the past. 'Whoever considers the past and the present will readily observe that all cities and all peoples are and ever have been animated by the same desires and the same passions; so that it is easy, by diligent study of the past, to foresee what is likely to happen in the future in any republic, and to apply those remedies that were used by the ancients, or not finding any that were used by them, to devise new ones from the similarity of the events. But as such considerations are neglected or not understood by most of those who read, or, if understood by these, are unknown by those who govern, it follows that the same troubles generally recur in all republics.' Machiavelli, then, will bridge the gap by putting the experience of the ancients at the disposal of the moderns, providing political analogies for the statesmen in the same way that Erasmus, in his *Adages*, provided metaphors for the man of letters. He admits that we do not know the whole truth about the past, that the sources are partial and subjective; he admits that the past often seems better than it was because we are not moved by fear or hatred when we read past events as we are when we think about current ones, but these admissions do not blunt his main thesis: the statesman can be taught from the past how to behave today.

This is the novelty of the work, to which Nardi alludes, and which Machiavelli states in so many words: 'I have resolved to follow a new route, which has not yet been followed by anyone.' That is, not to deduce the rules of political behaviour and constitutional reform by reference to first principles—the ideal man is such and such, therefore his political environ-

ment must be such and such—but from the actual conduct of men; to learn about statecraft not from philo-
sophy but from history. And he was progressive in his
looking on Roman history less as a matter for genea-
logical self-congratulation—a common humanist point
of view—as a spur for the flanks of the weak and erring
present.

But a knowledge of history, he emphasizes, while it
can help statesmen, cannot preserve states; that depends in part on character. No advice can sustain a
society that is pusillanimous and corrupt. One cause of
the inability of statesmen to use the lessons of antiquity
is that the moderns are effeminate as well as ignorant,
and this 'makes them regard the maxims of the ancients
as inhuman or impossible of application.' Christian
sentiment, in fact, gets in the way. We need the
strength *not* to turn the other cheek, the courage *not*
to grant the benefit of the doubt. The main failing of
contemporaries was that they were not prepared to
make sacrifices for their liberty, and this, he claimed,
was due in part to their religion. For Machiavelli,
religion was an institution that educated men, condi-
tioned them in a certain way. Because its influence was
deeper and subtler than that which any statesman
could exert, the founders of religions were greater than
the founders of states. He was not concerned with
truth; religions were to be judged in terms of their
social effects. Thus Mohammedanism was of greater
assistance to the statesman than Christianity, because
it made men warlike. Pagan religion celebrated men
of action, while Christianity lauded the humble and
contemplative man—or, rather, had come to lose its
original vigour because men 'have interpreted our reli-

gion according to the promptings of indolence rather than those of virtue'. This lethargic, cloister-stricken Christianity had stifled man's love of liberty. It followed that statesmen could not ignore religion; the binding force of a non-rational organization was needed to supplement that of a rational one; fear of God should fill the gaps that reason might find in the laws.

This conviction that religion can be used to medicine the body politic is part of Machiavelli's dynamic approach to his subject as a whole. He believed in omens—it would, indeed, have been unscientific not to; there was plenty of evidence, much of it from classical sources, to support the connection between heavenly portents and earthly crises—but he did not believe in surrender to the ominous; no situation was so threatening that man was absolved from trying to alter it. As in *The Prince*, he forestalled the objection that men's lives were dominated by Fortune. He admits her power, but says that as men cannot tell what she intends they should never despair; sometimes, indeed, she chastens in order more fully to bless. And he speaks as a true intellectual when he declares that Fortune can be tamed by knowledge. Political affairs, he declares in Chapter 30 of Book Two, 'will continue to fluctuate until some ruler shall arise who is so great an admirer of antiquity as to be able to govern so that Fortune may not have occasion, with every revolution of the sun, to display her influence and power'.

The first lesson of politics is self-reliance. Don't rely on God, he advises the statesman, don't give in to fortune, and don't let precautions taken at a distance be a substitute for resolute preparation at the centre. He criticizes the statesmen who trusts in anything but, ultimately, his own right arm. Opposition to an enemy, for instance, must be based on a citizen army protecting the country's heart : it is irresponsible to rely on diplomacy, on subsidies, on hiring mercenaries, on trying to retain the enemy at the frontiers of your state ; the use of gunpowder has not made so much difference that the personal qualities that made the Roman soldier great are no longer those on which victory depends. The only safeguard for a state is a disciplined citizenry, trained for war, putting the state's welfare before its own, and a leadership that applies with resolution lessons learned from the past. There is no need to repine at living in an age of crises ; indeed, a sense of necessity is needed to spur men to their best endeavours. A lasting peace is hardly to be expected ; situations change, men's natures are changeable ; flux is normal. It is unprofitable, even, to try to prevent all political unrest in the state itself. To keep the state alive and vital the citizens must be given a degree of responsibility and power, and this means that they may try to abuse it. But the risk must be faced ; to be tranquil is to be feeble ; a degree of social volatility is necessary for greatness. A constitution should canalize energies, not anaesthetize them.

Machiavelli felt the abuses of his time too personally to be a Utopian : he was nearer in temperament to Savonarola than to Sir Thomas More. Florence herself, while a prey to needless luxury, lack of martial spirit, and factiousness, was not in so bad a state as Milan, or Naples, where the people were too corrupt for liberty to be eventually restored, but matters were still bad enough to justify Machiavelli's use of the *Discourses* as a pulpit. Burningly he expressed his nostalgia for the hard but glorious life of Rome, and his disgust for the luxurious but shameful life of the present. He wanted men's characters to be reformed, corrupt citizens to be made into good ones. This could be done, in time, by the salutary disciplines of religion and the militia, but these institutions, he recognized, might need for a while to be controlled by a prince.

Machiavelli's own preference for a republican constitution comes out clearly enough in the *Discourses*. It would have been odd if it had not. Florentines compared themselves favourably, even in the days of Lorenzo the Magnificent, to the lesser breeds without the republican law. When the Medici returned in 1512 Florence remained a republic, and up to the time of Machiavelli's writing the *Discourses* they had not shown themselves too covetous of sole power. If Machiavelli appears to waver between an admiration now for republics, now for a prince, it is because republics, when dealing with the outside world, behaved like 'princes', or ought to, acting swiftly, and as one man, and because he believed that republics sometimes needed the stimulus of a reforming prince. The emphasis placed on republics in the *Discourses* does not point to a change of heart since *The Prince*. When he comes to comment on the behaviour of princes in the former work, he identifies himself with them readily enough and gives them advice. He speaks openly to all grades of authority, conscious that each has a part to play and could do it better if properly advised. He never thought, nor did his contemporaries think, in such terms as : should Florence be governed by a republican constitution or by an absolute prince? He was concerned with : what qualities should our republic show the outside world?, and how can our sick state have its vital tone restored? The answers to both questions involved a study of princes, but they did not envisage a choice which would lead to lasting princely rule. Republics that had run down might need princes to wind them up again, so the comprehensive writer on politics must include advice for princes. This does not conflict with Machiavelli's conviction that the greatest political glory is to found a republic, the greatest shame to establish a tyranny. The true glory lies not in triumphing over but in reforming a state, 'for certainly the heavens cannot afford a man a greater opportunity for glory, nor could man desire a better one'. And he goes further than this: 'If reformation calls for the resignation of princely authority itself, then both glory and security demand that the prince should voluntarily retire.' Revolutionary as this suggestion may seem, it was not whispered secretly in some conspiratorial cellar, but written out plain for Medicean partisans to read (as they had probably heard it discussed), and in 1519 or 1520 he was to offer the same advice, even more radically phrased, to the Medici themselves. It was based on the same assumption that Savonarola had made in his small treatise of 1498 on Florence's constitution: the people of Florence were too volatile, too covetous of their liberties, to tolerate what was theoretically the best constitutional form—the sole rule of a good man.

Machiavelli's point of view was idealistic—it was not likely that the Medici, or any other rulers, would in fact abdicate when they saw the common good demanded it—but it was not abstract; he was interested less in the ends of government than in the revolutions that made them possible; he was interested in the strains and stresses that precede completeness. Living in a period of crisis, he studied the past for the lessons to be learned from its own crises: more important to him than the Roman Republic or Empire at their height was the moment when the edge of one ground against the edge of the other, when Caesar's selfish greatness called for the dagger of Brutus.

Throughout his life Machiavelli oversimplified issues and presented them too much in terms of black and white. But at least the issues were live ones, they were within the compass of immediate action. To the very end of this long work, which occupied two years or more, the tone remains urgent and down-to-earth. In Chapter 41 of Book Three, returning to the question of fraud, he puts the 'Machiavellian attitude' in brief: 'Where the very safety of the country depends on the resolution to be taken, no considerations of justice or injustice, humanity or cruelty, nor of glory or shame, should be allowed to prevail. But putting all other considerations aside, the only question should be, "What course will save the life and liberty of the country?"'

The circle of the Rucellai provided Machiavelli with congenial friends; he wrote to one of them, Lodovico Alamanni, who was in Rome, on December 17th, 1517, describing the plans for a journey to Flanders which he and some of the others were planning. It provided him with confidence in his literary powers. He was listened to and praised. In the same letter he complained at being left out of the roll-call of notable contemporaries at the end of Ariosto's great work. 'I have been reading Ariosto's *Orlando Furioso*, and certainly the whole poem is beautiful, in places really remarkable fine. If he is there, remember me to him, and tell him that the only thing that pains me is that having referred to so many poets he has left me out like a dog, but that I shall not serve him in my *Asino* as he has served me in his *Orlando*.'

The possibility of having his verses read does not necessarily make an author into a better poet, but a dramatist works best with the bait and challenge of an actual production. Machiavelli had already written one play, *Andria*, which was hardly more than an exercise in translation from Terence's *The Woman of Andros,* but it was not until 1518 that he wrote a play that demonstrated his true originality. *Mandragola* was a brilliant work for the stage, and though there is no record of an actual performance being mooted until April 1520, it is very likely that it had by then been acted, or, at least read, in the Gardens. We know of two productions in the next few years, one as far afield as Venice, and one in Florence for which the scenery was painted by Bastiano da Sangallo and Andrea del Sarto.

Though virtually unperformed since Machiavelli's own lifetime, at least in its original form, the play has never lacked admirers. For Voltaire, it was 'perhaps worth more than all the comedies of Aristophanes'. For Macaulay, it was 'superior to the best of Goldoni, and inferior only to the best of Molière'. But these were judgments on the literary merits of the piece. More important were the comments of Goldoni himself, whose ideas of stagecraft were influenced by Machiavelli. During a holiday from the ecclesiastical college in Pavia he was lent the play, rather unexpectedly, by a canon, who had found it among the possessions of one of his colleagues. 'I devoured it on the first reading', Goldoni wrote in his memoirs, 'and I perused it at least ten times afterwards. It was neither the free style nor the scandalous intrigue of the piece which fascinated me : its lubricity even disgusted me, and I could perceive that the abuse of confession was a heinous crime both in the eye of God and man; but it was the first comedy of character which had ever fallen into my hands, and I was quite enchanted with it. How desirable it would have been had the Italian authors continued after this comedy', he went on, 'to draw their characters from nature instead of indulging in romantic intrigues.'

This is the strength of the play, the quality that enables it to support its own life on the stage ; without being a formless reproduction of nature, the play shows people of flesh and blood in a real city at a definite time involved in a scheme which, for all its absurdity, is made to appear credible. Its appeal did not depend on classical reminiscence, nor on the virtuosity of specially endowed actors : it spoke to all classes; and its subsequent neglect was due not to its quality but to fashion—first a canalizing of bourgeois comedy into the *scenarii* of the *Commedia dell' Arte,* then a preference, as far as bawdy was concerned, for what was suggested rather than stated.

This is not to say that *Mandragola* was independent of all models. The plot is an ingenious and crude practical joke of the sort familiar to generations of readers of Florentine *Novelle.* Callimaco, a Florentine youth, is in love with Lucrezia, the young wife of

Messer Nicia, a pompous old lawyer. She is virtuous and strictly guarded. How is he to seduce her? The play provides the answer. On the advice of Ligurio, an unscrupulous adventurer, Callimaco poses as a doctor; Messer Nicia longs for children, the promise of them is the one bait he is prepared to swallow. The false doctor offers him a potion for his wife made from mandrake—the Mandragola of the title. But there is a difficulty, he says; whoever is the first to sleep with a woman who has taken such a potion dies. If some stranger, however, can be found to draw off the poison, then all will be well. Messer Nicia is won over, but two problems remain : to persuade Lucrezia to accept the plan, and to make sure that it is Callimaco himself who, as the 'stranger', finds his way to his mistress's bed. Lucrezia's protests are borne down by her mother, Sostrata, and Fra Timoteo, her confessor; Callimaco succeeds, gains her love and, next morning, the friar takes them all into church in a mood of general self-congratulation—gulled and gulling alike. There is no conflict, no real suspense; the plot is an anecdote, an ingenious smoking-room story, told with pace and pungency and without sentiment.

The form of the play, its construction, owes much to Roman comedy, as do some of the characters: Ligurio, the parasite, for instance, and Sostrata, the fussy, worldly-wise mother. Messer Nicia anticipates the Dottore of the *Commedia dell' Arte*, and in the same way Siro, the puzzled and good-humoured servant, looks back to Boccaccio's bumpkins and forward to Arlecchino. Lucrezia, too, might take her place among other gentle heroines of the *Decameron*, too intelligent to be always virtuous. They are types and, in so far as they serve the action, they behave typically. But because they also serve the mood, the specifically Machiavellian temper of the play, they are also original. Ligurio, the play's taut spring, forcing all the wheels to rotate until the alarm is over and the lady won, is the man who, now by insinuation and aside, now by direct assault, shakes Fortune into submission —obeying rules for the man of action preached by Machiavelli elsewhere. As one after the other the characters are drawn into the light of the play's main problem—how to perform a bad act for a good end— their conventional aspect is left in the shadows : we see Lucrezia trapped and shamed, her mother's good nature defining itself as moral obliquity, Fra Timoteo allowing his lack of scruple to lead him down a path paved with ducats. Messer Nicia adjusts himself to the rape of his wife by the stranger when he hears that the king of France has done the same, and lends himself with infantile enthusiasm to every turn of the plot that is to bring about his own cuckoldom.

The play was printed almost at once, and Machiavelli wrote for the press a prologue which stressed that in spite of its light-hearted nature it was not written by a happy man. Machiavelli since 1513 had had a picture of himself as a man who has from time to time to relieve his unhappiness by playing the jester. On April 16th of that year he had included these verses in a letter to Vettori : 'And if I sometimes laugh or sing, I do it as I have no other way to ease my bitter grief.' The *Mandragola* prologue begins by describing the plot, then turns to introspection in a similar vein.

And if this seems too light and frivolous
For one who likes to be thought serious,
Forgive him: for he tries with idle dreams
To make the hour less bitter than it seems.
—Bitter, for he can turn no other way
To show a higher worth, do what he may;
For graver themes
He sees no chance of patronage or pay.

The payment he expects is jeers and spite,
For everyone to damn his work outright.
Such treatment is a proof the present day
Declines from ancient worth in every way.
And who will strain, when all they get is scorn,
To achieve a work of art?—A work that's born
To fade away,
Hidden in mist, or by the tempest torn.

But he who thinks this author can be wrung
By malice, or be made to hold his tongue,
I warn him: this man is malicious too;
Malice, indeed, his earliest art, and through
The length and limits of all Italy
He owes respect to none; though I agree
He'll fawn and do
Service to richer, smarter folk than he.

Even the friendly patronage of the Oricellari gardens was not, apparently, without its sting.

Among the subjects debated there, as in every literary circle in Italy, was the merits of the vernacular. Machiavelli's *Dialogue on our Language* appears to have been a continuation of such a debate in writing on returning to his study at S. Andrea. He refers to a recent discussion, one of those originating in a visit paid to the gardens in 1513 by Giangiorgio Trissino, the discoverer of Dante's *De Vulgari Eloquentia,* as to whether the language used by the great writers of the past should be called Florentine, Tuscan, or Italian, and, putting his own opinion in the form of a letter to an unnamed friend, he begins by claiming that greater respect is due to a man's *patria* even than to his family, and that its good name should be even more zealously guarded. For this reason he is going to demonstrate that the language of Dante, Petrarch, and Boccaccio was that of Florence, and that, as a result, wherever the best Italian is employed, it derives from the Florentine tongue.

Among the problems set by this aim was the task of persuading Dante himself to admit that he wrote in Florentine, not in *curiale*—that is, the language common to all the courts of Italy. He achieves this by means of a passage of dialogue which is similar in tone to the natural, vigorous dialogue of *Mandragola.* Machiavelli's knowledge of Dante is clear from numerous quotations and allusions throughout his prose writings and his poetry (a passage from Dante quoted in this *Dialogue* recurs in the Prologue to *Mandragola*), and he adopts an easy, not to say brusque, manner with his hero. Dante has already admitted some of his points when Machiavelli challenges him outright :

N. Why do you say you aren't speaking Florentine, then? However, I want to convince you with book in hand, by comparing texts. So let us read your work together with the *Morgante.*[1] Read here.

[1] The *Morgante Maggiore* of the Florentine poet Luigi Pulci, begun about 1460, first published in full in 1483.

D. 'Nel mezzo del cammin di nostra vita
   Mi ritrovai per una selva oscura
   Che la diretta via era smarrita.'

N. That's enough. Now read a bit of the *Morgante*.

D. Where?

N. Where you like. Read at random.

D. Here you are, then.
   'Non chi comincia ha meritato, è scritto
   Nel tuo santo Vangel, benigno Padre.'

N. Now then, what difference is there between your language and that?

D. Not much.

N. I don't think there is any.

D. There's something about this, perhaps.

N. What? D. This *chi* is too Florentine.

N. The joke is really on you; don't you say yourself 'Io non so *chi* tu sia...'?

D. That's true. I was mistaken.

And Machiavelli goes on to point out that Dante had so far taken advantage of the Florentine idiom that he had exploited even its seamy side, 'for art can never divorce itself altogether from nature'.

Another work that probably dates from the years 1515 to 1520 is *Belfagor,* Machiavelli's only independent short story as opposed to the long anecdotes he had included in letters. This *Fable,* as it was headed in Machiavelli's manuscript, neatly combined two popular themes: wives are an affliction too terrible to be born even by devils, and the craft of a peasant can outwit the infernal powers. The story opens with Pluto resolving to discover the truth of the assertion made by the majority of damned souls that they owed their misery to their wives. After taking council with his princes, he sent a devil, Belfagor, into the world to marry and verify the facts. Belfagor, dispatched with an allowance of one hundred thousand ducats, chose Florence for his inquiry because it was the best place to turn an investment to good account, and was not particularly religious (this latter point was cancelled in the manuscript), and married a noble wife who proceeded to ruin him by her caprice and extravagance.

Before long he was bankrupt and forced to flee from his creditors. He was saved from their pursuit by a peasant, Gianmatteo, whose fortune he promised to make in return by 'possessing' girls and then quitting them when Gianmatteo pretended to exorcise him. He did this twice, and Gianmatteo became rich on the proceeds—but also so famous that when the king of France sent for him to cure his daughter, he was forced to go in spite of Belfagor's threat to do no more for him. On his arrival in France the king told him that the penalty of failure would be death. Gianmatteo nevertheless staged the exorcism with much ceremony, including a concealed brass band. He approached the girl and begged Belfagor to leave her. The devil refused. Gianmatteo then signed to the band which struck up with horrid din. Terrified, Belfagor asked what was happening. 'It's your wife come to find you!' answered the peasant, and Belfagor at once left the girl and fled back to hell and bore witness to the miseries of married life.

To all the literary success of these years, the *Mandragola* Prologue could stand as introduction. They were also years of personal distress, of disappointed ambition and of poverty. Strung through them are letters to Giovanni Vernaccia, each sounding a note of grief and futility. It was probably during these years that he dedicated an Italian version of an ancient poem, 'On Opportunity', to Filippo Nerli, which comments ruefully on the man who talks and talks but grasps at opportunity too late. But the only opportunity that came during these years was a very small one : an invitation from a group of Florentine merchants to go to Genoa to protect interests of theirs which were imperilled by the bankruptcy of a creditor. He grasped it, but it can have done little to reduce his nostalgia for the great days of Rome, when, as he had written in Chapter 25 of the *Discourses*, 'poverty was never allowed to stand in the way of the achievement of any rank or honour, and virtue and merit were sought for under whatever roof they dwelt'.

CHAPTER NINE

The Art of War *and Medici Patronage:*
1519 – 1521

MACHIAVELLI'S fortunes improved during the years
1520 and 1521; he continued to be encouraged by the
circle of the Oricellari Gardens, and he began to be
patronized at last by the Medici, who, while remaining
reluctant to grant him any political responsibility,
commissioned him to write the *History of Florence.*

Lorenzo, the second and indifferent dedicatee of *The
Prince,* died in May 1519. He had removed himself
farther and farther from day-to-day contact with his
fellow citizens, and there had been fears that, egged
on by his imperious and caste-conscious mother, Alfon-
sina, he was planning to make himself supreme in
Florence. At his funeral, when the citizens were
obediently clad in mourning, one man appointed himself a symbol of their inner relief: at the head of the
grave procession of guild officials walked a young man
carrying roses in his hand and dressed from head to
foot in scarlet.

Lorenzo's successor as leader of the family interest
was a man for whom scarlet was a working dress.
Cardinal Giulio dei Medici soon cooled the factious
temperature of the city by showing himself to be acces-
sible, liberal, but modest in his public and private
expenditure. As another brushstroke in his cautious

self-portrait in the style of Lorenzo the Magnificent, he let it be known that he intended to seek out and patronize men of merit. He was already familiar with the political views Machiavelli had expressed to Vettori in 1514 and was now prepared to overlook his anti-Medicean services to the Soderini republic, and welcomed him when he was presented by some of his Oricellari friends in March 1520. The leading figure in this reconciliation was Lorenzo Strozzi, brother of the Filippo Strozzi who had married Clarice dei Medici and it was to him that Machiavelli dedicated *The Art of War,* which was finished in the autumn of 1520 and published under Machiavelli's own careful supervision in the following August.

The book was a labour of love. It enabled Machiavelli to celebrate publicly his fascination with the technical aspects of war, and provided a more spacious setting for a theme anticipated in both *The Prince* and the *Discourses*: that good laws depend on a sound military organization. For Machiavelli the organization of an army had a double purpose: to repel the enemy without and to reform the citizens within. For this reason *The Art of War,* while dealing with the whole business of war from levying troops to distributing the spoils after battle, from fundamentals like the art of fortification to notes on the use of drums, is the essential wing of a political tryptich: *Prince—Discourses—Art of War.*

The scene is set in the Oricellari Gardens, and into its pleasant walks, soft grass, and shady benches under the trees, Machiavelli does not hesitate to introduce a jarring note. Fabrizio Colonna, a professional soldier, is brought into the gardens by Cosimo Rucellai and asked what he thinks of them. Instead of praising them he deplores that they were ever made, for they symbolize a retreat from public responsibility to private self-indulgence. Cosimo agrees in principle, but explains what his grandfather's motives had been. 'I do not believe', he tells Colonna, 'that there was any man of his time who detested a soft and delicate way of life more than he did, or was a greater friend to that sternness of life you praise. Nevertheless, he found it impossible either for himself or his sons to practise it; for such was the corruption of the age he lived in that if anyone had spirit enough to deviate from the common manner of living he would have been universally slandered and despised.' And he went on to say that his grandfather was therefore discouraged from imitating the example of the ancients. In reply, Colonna says that he does not expect the copying of the ancients to go to extremes, but that it should involve such things 'as would be suited to the present times, which I think might very well be established if they were introduced by some man of authority in the state.' And when Cosimo asks him to name them, Colonna begins with two that were very near Machiavelli's heart—'to honour and reward virtue; not to despise poverty'. The rest were 'to keep up good order and discipline in armies, to oblige fellow citizens to love one another, to live without factions, and to prefer the good of the public to any private interest'. Above all, Machiavelli emphasizes, the false modern antithesis between the civilian and the military life must be broken down. The citizen must no longer scorn the soldier and the soldier despise the civilian. Ideally, the soldier is the citizen in another guise. Machia-

velli threw himself into the technical side of his
subject with abandon ('I am ready. The signal is
given. Do you not hear our artillery?' cries Colonna,
describing an imaginary battle), but he never forgot for
long that the fundamental requirement in a soldier is a
resolute state of mind, that the softening effect of
Christianity must be reversed, that gunpowder must
not be allowed to dethrone valour, that Fortune, with
her brow heavy-knit with disasters, can still be out-
stared.

His basic concern with civic morale made him
press the claims of a militia, the best type of army in
spite of the dismal showing its units had made at Prato
in 1512. In order to have a real expert whose opinions
would carry weight, he was forced to use a professional
soldier as hero of *The Art of War,* but Colonna is made
to protest that he himself thinks the use of mercenary
arms is 'a very corrupt custom', and to explain that he
only hires himself out to others because he has so few
subjects of his own. Indeed, the more Machiavelli was
preoccupied with the importance of improving the
civic tone of Florence by means of the militia, the less
inclined he was to scrutinize the evidence he used to
prove its military usefulness. He assumed, wrongly,
that the conquering armies of Rome had always been
composed of citizen-soldiers; he quoted the example of
the German cities without taking into account the fact
that they employed mercenaries for all but defensive
purposes, of the German *lanzknechts* without pointing out that for the most part they fought in small paid
bands under the leadership of some country land-
owner, and of the Swiss who were notorious for thinking of fee first and cause second. On the other hand, he

underestimated the skill and faithfulness of contemporary mercenary troops and their leaders. Italy could provide as many examples of faithful condottiere leaders as treacherous ones, but the militia was to be allowed no rivals. Thinking, again, primarily of the militia's political role, Machiavelli not only repeated the precautionary clauses built into the ordinances of 1506 and 1512, but went further, emphasizing that the keen volunteer should be ignored, as he was likely to put delight in war before obedience to the civil authority; the ideal militia-man should be neither over-keen nor sluggish in his wish to serve. In his effort to produce an army that would be safe politically, Machiavelli was rendering it ineffective from a military point of view, and he sustained his prejudice by an extremely selective use of classical analogies. A militia, for instance, could not be trained highly enough to use pikes, but this mattered little; the Romans with their individualistic weapons of sword and buckler had beaten the Macedonian phalanxes, and in the same way the modern militia could defeat the massed pikes of a professional army.

The Roman soldier was, besides, a model of diligence and sobriety for all time. In a typically loaded question Colonna was asked, 'Did the Romans ever allow women or gambling in camp, as we do now?' and the answer, of course, was 'no'. There was a need for a radical change of heart in both subjects and rulers. It is in *The Art of War,* the most technical of his works, that Machiavelli's moral indignation sounds most scathing. 'Before our Italian princes were scourged by the Ultramontanes', he cried near the end of the work, 'they thought it enough for princes to write a handsome letter, or return a pointed answer; to excell in drollery and repartee; to embroider a fraud; and to set themselves off with jewels and gold; to eat and sleep in greater magnificence than their neighbours; to surround themselves with every indulgence; to keep up a haughty kind of state and grind the faces of their subjects, to abandon themselves to indolence, to give military offices to favourites, to neglect and despise merit of every kind, to have their words treated like those of an oracle—not seeing (weak wretches as they were) that by such conduct they were exposing themselves to the mercy of the first invader.' If only, he goes on, our rulers would read about the great heroic figures of antiquity they would surely reform themselves and their states. The weapon is to hand: it is the formation of national armies and the employment of the technical lessons described in this book. Where there is a desire to learn there is hope. Italy has already seen the revitalization of poetry, painting, and sculpture; indeed, it seems destined to waken talents from the grave; might not the art of war be one of them? And on this optimistic note closes a work which sometimes does greater credit to Machiavelli's heart than to his head.

In July 1520, when *The Art of War* was probably complete or nearly so, Machiavelli was asked to go to Lucca to settle disputes arising, as in the case of the Genoese affair, from a bankruptcy. This time the matter was more complex, and he was sent not by a private merchant but by the government—the Signoria and the cardinal. The matter was complicated; there were many legal formalities to be observed, many officials to be consulted. The settlement dragged on till

September. Machiavelli used what leisure he had to examine the constitution and the history of Lucca, and to write a *Summary of Lucchese Affairs* about the one and *The Life of Castruccio Castracani* from the other.

The *Summary* was a brief survey of the way in which Lucca was governed. It was written for the benefit of someone unnamed—possibly the Cardinal himself; the *Discourses* had shown Machiavelli's interest in constitutional forms, and the Cardinal, who was interested in getting suggestions for a model Florentine constitution even from 'liberal' intellectuals, had been, on Leo X's advice, thinking of extending some sort of employment to him. This suggestion is at least consistent with Machiavelli's conclusion that though the Lucchese constitution worked, 'anyone organizing a republic should not imitate it'. That Machiavelli was no radical, harking back to the days of the republic of Savonarola, or even of Soderini, is clear from one of the few passages of generalization in the work. The government of Lucca lacked weight, he claimed, because the brief terms of office and the numerous exclusions due to class jealousies compelled the nomination of men of small account. So it was continually necessary to take the advice of private citizens, 'which is not usual in well-organized republics where the greatest number elect to office, the medium number gives advice, the minority executes. . . . Thus did the people, Senate and consuls of Rome; thus do now in Venice the Grand Council, the Senate and the Signoria'. He thus censures, by implication, the promotion of men of small account to executive posts. On the other hand, he supports the need for a Great Council of some sort. Machiavelli is no more a sycophant than he was in 1512. Nor is he, on the other hand, a more extreme republican than he was then.

Castruccio Castracani is a historical fantasy based on the career of a foundling (*b.* 1281) who by political ruthlessness and military genius became lord of Lucca and half Tuscany. What drew Machiavelli to write a historical work at all is not clear. He probably knew that Giulio intended to commission him to write something, he might have known that it was to be a history, and this might have prompted him—his head still full of the art of war—to write about the most celebrated soldier in the history of Lucca. He was in a communicative vein, we know; Nerli complained on August 1st of having had a letter from him which began by promising to be brief and then ran on for two crammed pages. It was, besides, a congenial theme. Castruccio had much in common with Cesare Borgia, and Machiavelli, using sources as guides, could nevertheless invent freely the links between what was uppermost in his mind : war, its expertise and stratagems ; the need for a resolute but responsible leader; and the sharp division between public and private morality—the vengeful and truce-breaking Castruccio abstains from marriage rather than break his word to a dying man. Certainly *Castruccio* was not written for Cardinal Giulio, or for the eyes of the officials of the university who would have to support his appointment as state historiographer ; he was careless of dates, invented facts and attributed to his hero a string of old saws which a professional audience would know at once to be bogus. It was sent to two friends of the Oricellari Gardens, Buondelmonti and Alamanni, in an impetuous and playful vein : If you expect history from *me,* beware that this is not the sort of thing you get.

It contains many of the ingredients of fashionable historiography : detailed descriptions of military affairs ; internal party strife ; the deeds of a great man ; a dying oration. It contains reflections of familiar Machiavellian themes, and suggests a growing moderation, for instance in the death-bed assertion of Castruccio that had he known that Fortune would have cut him off so unexpectedly, he would have striven for less, and left behind him a smaller but safer patrimony; but it would be hazardous to press any of its apparent morals to extremes. *Castruccio* was not meant to be taken too seriously. Buondelmonti wrote on September 6th to thank Machiavelli for the manuscript and said that he and several of the others had seen it, including Iacopo Nardi, himself an historian, and that they had all enjoyed it, though they remained a little puzzled. They did not see the point of the sayings attributed to Castruccio, for instance. But, by and large, their conclusion was that the straightforward history in it made it clear that he should proceed from this *modello* to a major work ; 'this history' was the phrase, and it surely referred to the project for a history of Florence.

The commission came on November 8th, but the negotiations leading up to it had been known to Machiavelli, at least in part : he had even drawn up a draft contract and submitted it to a relation who was the registrar of the university. It suggested that the agreement should bind him 'to write the annals or rather history of the things done by the state and city of Florence, from whatever time seems most suitable to him, and in either the Latin or Tuscan tongue, as he shall choose'. The final contract followed the general lines of the draft, but used the formula '*inter alia ad componendum annalia et cronacas florentinas, et alia faciendum*', which gave the university more power over him than he had suggested, and avoided the term history, which could be extended more readily than the more old-fashioned annals and chronicles, to cover the interpretation, as well as the bare record, of facts. The contract brought a measure of security, for he received an annual fee which amounted to a little more than half his pre-1512 salary.

Before he could begin this task, however, he was asked by the cardinal to submit an advice on the best form of government for Florence. He was not the first to be approached; Buondelmonti and Alamanni had already submitted their views. Giulio's motives were mixed. He felt a genuine need to sound opinion after the recent suspicion of Lorenzo; he thought it tactful to put up a show of co-operation with some of the more influential Florentine intellectuals; and there was the fact that as the two heads of the family—himself and the Pope—could, as ecclesiastics, have no heirs, the direct line would end with their deaths. The future, as a result, was uncertain.

Machiavelli replied with a *Discourse on Florentine Affairs after the Death of Lorenzo*. Once more he showed a lack of understanding of the mentality of the great families which allowed him to give his academic approach to politics a loose rein. He took it for granted that the deaths of Giulio and Leo would spell the end of the Medici domination, not taking into account the claims of the younger branch of the family or the party of Medicean supporters who had been strong enough to undermine the republic before 1512 and were now more strongly entrenched and committed than ever. Machiavelli's main thesis was one that he had already advanced in Chapter 9, Book One, of the *Discourses,* that while reform should be the work of one man, the reformed state should be restored to the hands of the many.

The *Discourse on Florentine Affairs* was intended for the eyes of Giulio and Leo, and Machiavelli begins by assuming that they are more inclined to strengthen the popular than the autocratic element in the present constitution, no reputation being more glorious than that of the legislator who improves the constitution of a republic. On the other hand, he accepts that they will want to preserve their own power and abdicate only by death. He faces the task, then, of preparing for a fully republican constitution while preserving Medici domination during the lifetimes of the cardinal and the Pope. This could be done by re-educating the popular element in the constitution through the restoration of a Great Council, and by subjecting all the elections to important offices to Medici control. When that control came to be removed, the constitution should then be capable of looking after itself. His main assumption, in fact, enabled him both to eat his cake and have it; to legislate for a republic, while providing means to preserve Medici domination during the lifetime of his patrons.

He begins by making it clear that the clock cannot be put back to the previous century. The Medici régime was insecure then, and the republican temper of the citizens had subsequently become more insistent. There must be a show of liberty, which would later become real. The best constitution (as he had suggested in his essay on Lucca) would consist of a Great Council to elect officers, a Senate to deliberate and a Signoria to execute; the Great Council to consist of 600–1,000 citizens of the lower responsible class; the Senate of 200, 160 coming from the middle, 40 from the lower class; the Signoria to be recruited, for three months, from a body of 65 (53 from the upper, 12 from the middle class), one of whom would become Gonfalonier of Justice. Thus each interest would have a voice in the body above it, the lower class in the Senate and the middle class in the Signoria. To give greater assurance to the people that power was not being concentrated at the top, a representative of the people's local administration was to sit with the Signoria, and there was to be a special court of accusations, before which government officials could be denounced by any injured party—a safety-valve which had been, like much else in this programme, suggested in the *Discourses*. The Medici were to control this structure by appointing the 65 and the 200 and the Gonfalonier, and though the consequent elections would come from the newly instituted Great Council, the Medici could be sure that only their own candidates were successful by appointing assessors who would be pledged, in strict secrecy, to arrange matters so that the lots fell only upon 'safe' men. Towards the end of this *Discourse* Machiavelli confessed the nature of his own stake in this best-of-both-worlds scheme. After repeating that the greatest good a man can do is to help his country, he said : 'This glory has been so much cherished by men who have no other aim than glory, that not having been able to found a Republic in deed, they have made one in writing, as did Aristotle, Plato and many others, who wished to show the world that if they have not been able to found a Republic themselves, as did Lycurgus and Solon, it is not on account of their ignorance, but their lack of power.'

In April 1521 a prospect of power offered itself. Soderini, who had been suffered to return to Rome, and who had already offered Machiavelli a post at Ragusa, which he had refused, wrote from Rome on April 13th to offer him the post of chief agent, or secretary (the exact status was not made clear), to the condottiere and territorial magnate Prospero Colonna, whose cousin Fabrizio was the hero of *The Art of War*. The salary was to be more than four times what he was getting as state historiographer. Soderini urged him to accept, and the chance of becoming adviser to a prince, even a very minor one, must have been tempting. But it would have meant leaving Florence, his family, his friends and his new-found security; he decided that it was better to roll stones for the Medici than become a rolling stone himself.

The next stone the Medici gave him, however, was one that might well have made him regret his decision. He was asked to go to Carpi, near Modena, to persuade the General Chapter of the Friars Minor, then sitting there, to agree to a separation of the Florentine members of the order from the others, so that they could be made subject to a stricter rule. On arrival he found a second commission, even less flattering to his self-respect; it was from the Florentine wool guild, who were responsible for selecting preachers for the cathedral in Lent, and charged him with securing the services of one of the brothers at Carpi.

On his way to the monastery he visited Francesco Guicciardini, then governing Reggio and Modena for Leo X, and resident at Modena. Thus recommenced a contact that was to ripen acquaintance into friendship. When Machiavelli had arrived at Carpi and sent word back about the new commission he found waiting for him there, Guicciardini replied at once, on May 17th: 'Machiavelli *carissimo*. It has certainly been a wise decision on the part of the honourable consuls of the good guild to have entrusted you with the selection of a preacher; it is as if Pacchierotto, while he lived, or Ser Sano [a notorious homosexual] had been charged with selecting a fair and lively bride for a friend.' And he went on to say that if Machiavelli took to religion now, 'having always lived in the contrary way', he would be thought to be in his second childhood, and he ended by warning Machiavelli against the air of Carpi which had long had the reputation of turning men into liars.

Machiavelli replied that there was no danger of his becoming infected with religion. Indeed, he intended to depart from his brief by selecting not a preacher whose goodness would show the way to heaven but whose badness would point the way to hell. As for lying—he had nothing to learn in that art. 'For some time past I have never said what I believe, nor believe what I say, and if I do happen to speak the truth, I wrap it up in so many lies that it is difficult to get at it.' He ends by thanking Guicciardini for building up his prestige by sending a mounted messenger, and begs for another who might create even more effect among the friars.

Guicciardini, catching and sustaining Machiavelli's

mood, replied by dispatching a messenger with instructions to ride so fast that his shirt stood out from his
back, and provided him with 'some reports from
Zurich, which you can turn to good account by perus-
ing them or handing them round'. And he urged
Machiavelli to sow dissension among the friars and
set them at loggerheads. But he followed this flippant
letter with a serious one later in the day. 'When I read
your credentials as envoy of the Republic and of the
friars,' he wrote, 'and consider with how many kings,
dukes, and princes you have negotiated in other
times, I recall Lysander who, after so many victories
and triumphs, was given the job of distributing meat
to the very soldiers he had so gloriously commanded.'
He goes on to speak of Machiavelli's historical work,
and to say that he believed that even this mission might
be of some use, for in the three days of his stay Machiavelli 'will have got to the bottom of the Republic of
Sandals, and some opportunity would come of making
use of its structure, comparing or contrasting it with
one of your own systems'. It seems that Machiavelli's
reputation as a constitutional planner was based on
more than the *Discourse on Florentine Affairs*: probably on other blueprints discussed with his Oricellari
friends. Machiavelli wrote next day to stop Guicciardini sending any more messengers: the friars were
beginning to be suspicious and he did not want to lose
'the marvellous dishes and the glorious beds' which his
reputation had won, by straining the joke too far. The
mission, besides, was nearly over. In a day or two he
was in Modena on his way back. He had failed in both
respects: the friars decided that they were not com-

petent to decide on the issue of separation, and the preacher did not want to come to Florence.

Machiavelli settled down at home to work on his history of Florence while Italy prepared for war. In that same May 1521 Leo allied secretly with Charles V with the aim of driving the French once more from Italy, incorporating Parma and Piacenza in the papal states, and taking Ferrara. Hostilities began in August, and the papal-Spanish armies drove the French from northern Italy, though they left a few isolated pockets of resistance and a garrison under Lautrec in the castle of Milan itself. At this moment of triumph, Leo died on December 1st, and for the rest of the year the college of cardinals hesitated over the election of a successor. The fortunes of war began to swing the other way. Duke Francesco Maria della Rovere, expelled from Urbino by the Medici, returned there; the Duke of Ferrara recaptured most of the possessions that he had recently lost; Lautrec sallied out from Milan and attacked Parma, which was successfully, and extremely bravely, defended by Guicciardini, who had had Parma added to his governorship of Reggio and Modena. There was a chance of Cardinal Giulio becoming his brother's successor, but he was strongly opposed, and on January 9th the Fleming Adrian VI was elected. Meanwhile plots were being laid against the rule of the Medici in Florence itself. Machiavelli's career was once more in jeopardy.

CHAPTER TEN

Machiavelli's Last Years: 1522–1527

LITTLE is known about Machiavelli's activities in 1522, but the early months of that year were troubled by plots against the Medici, and it is doubtful if he was able to work readily at his history until the fortunes of the family that had commissioned it were settled. Cardinal Soderini was known to be planning a triumphal return for his family, using troops hired with French money; and Cardinal Giulio was sufficiently alarmed at this prospect, when it was still little more than rumour, to attempt a further consolidation of his power within Florence. Up to this time the influence of the Medici, though dominant, had not been signed and sealed into the city's constitution. Giulio's aim was to consolidate his own position, and to pay, or at least appear to pay, for this by making the basis of the constitution more popular. Accordingly, he offered to restore the Great Council in May, and encouraged, as he had done from time to time before, advice from individual citizens on the form the constitution should take.

Machiavelli made it clear that he had no sympathy with the machinations of his old protector and chief by sending in to Giulio a new version of the plan he had submitted in 1520, but it was soon clear that the Cardinal, though ready to accept advice from him and

from others, had no intention of acting on it. It was
doubted, moreover, whether he was in earnest over the
Great Council, and when he was given a pretext for
postponing its restoration by the advance of the
Soderini force towards Siena, suspicion hardened into
a definite plot. It originated in the group which had
been most prolific of constitutional suggestions and
most disillusioned by their rejection : Machiavelli's own
group, the Oricellari circle. The members of this coterie
had been divided after the death of Leo between those
who were personal friends of the Medici and were prepared for the family's continued predominance in the
city, and those who opposed it. Machiavelli, anxious
for liberty but prepared to wait during Giulio's lifetime,
represented a middle course. He was certainly against
changing the present régime by force : the longest
chapter in the *Discourses* had been devoted to decry-
ing conspiracies, and his personal fortunes, such as they
were, were bound up with those of Cardinal Giulio.
All the same, when a conspiracy to assassinate the Cardinal was formed under the leadership of his close
friends Buondelmonti and Alamanni, it was believed
—this is Nardi's opinion, and he was there to watch—
that Machiavelli's praise of republics and of the actions
of men who prepared the way for them had had the
effect of inclining the opinions of some of his associates
towards violence.

An attack on Giulio in Florence was planned to
coincide with the success of Soderini at Siena, and
when this failed it was called off, but correspondence
from Battista della Palla—the conspirators' agent in
Rome (also a friend of Machiavelli's)—was inter-

cepted and the plot was brought into the open. Buondelmonti and Alamanni were alerted in time and fled, but others were caught and executed after confessing their guilt under torture. At a blow, then, Machiavelli lost the company of the Oricellari circle, which was broken up by this crisis, and was on the brink of becoming involved as he had been in the Boscoli conspiracy. When the news reached him, not long after, that Piero Soderini had died on June 13th, he vented his anger and relief in an epigram which recalls the tone in which he had written of Boscoli and Capponi in 1513:

> *The night that Piero Soderini died*
> *His soul went to hell mouth, where Pluto cried,*
> *'There's no place, feeble soul, for you in Hades—*
> *Go off to Limbo, with the other babies!'*

—lines which reflected Machiavelli's dislike of Soderini's sitting-on-the-fence foreign policy before 1512, and his resentment at having had his career once more brought into jeopardy.

He retained, in fact, the favour of the Medici, and continued quietly working on *The History of Florence*. He had already studied Florentine history carefully when composing the *Discourses*. Thanks to the notes he had taken from chancery records while he was still in government employment, he could work at home in the country. The sources he used—the works of Giovanni Cavalcanti, Poggio, Bruni, and Biodo—were in print, or readily obtainable in manuscript copies, like the copy of the *Cronica fiorentina* ascribed to Minerbetti, which was lent to him with the owner's endorsement:

O Machiavelli, while you enjoy me,
Take care the lamp does not stain me.
Give me back soon, and keep me from the children.

The work went ahead slowly, but this was not so much due to the nature of his sources as to the difficulty of describing the gradual enslavement of Florence by the Medici in the fifteenth century in a book commissioned by the Medici family. He had discussed this problem with a newcomer to the Oricellari circle, who was to rival his fame as a political theorist, Donato Giannotti, and took it up again later with Guicciardini, to whom he wrote on August 30th, 1524, to say how much he wished he could come to tell him what passages might possibly give offence. Determined, moreover, not to give a straightforward annalistic treatment to his subject, but shape it to underline his favourite themes, he worked slowly, paying great attention to balance and style. The work was not brought up to the death of Lorenzo the Magnificent until early in 1525.

There seem to have been few interruptions, the only other literary preoccupations of these years being a long letter of advice to Raffaello Girolami in the autumn of 1522, and the writing of his play *Clizia* in 1524. Girolami was a young Florentine who was sent on a mission to Spain in October 1522. It was his first experience of diplomacy, and Machiavelli wrote him a long letter setting out the qualities and duties of a good ambassador, based on his own experience. It expresses his views on the subject better than any other source.

He begins by stressing the fact that it is a great compliment and honour to represent one's country abroad, and then gives the following advice : Get yourself a good reputation : you must be thought liberal, for instance, and honourable—not the sort of person who says one thing and thinks another. He admits that dissimulation will sometimes be necessary, and on those occasions it must be carried off as effectively as possible. Study the characters of the chief men at court, their tastes and their ambitions. Extract all the information you can by suiting your own habits to those of others, gambling, for instance, if others gamble; be careful to have a supply of information to give in exchange for theirs. The aim of your investigations of men and affairs is to be able to sum up a situation and its likely consequences, but—Machiavelli adds a piece of advice that indicates where his own voice is to be heard—when you write dispatches home, don't express your opinion too directly : use modest circumlocutions like 'sensible men here think that such and such will happen'.

In September 1523, Adrian VI died, and Machiavelli's patron, Cardinal Giulio, was elected Pope in the following month as Clement VII. His elevation meant that Florence became less free than ever. To some extent Giulio's tact and his genuine regard for Florentine interests had blurred the fact that the republic was run in all important respects from the Medici palace rather than from the Palazzo della Signoria. His removal to Rome should have meant, according to the idealists, that as no legitimate member of the main branch of the family was available, the city ought to be restored to the enjoyment of a full republican status. What in fact happened was that

Clement sent the young bastard sons of Giuliano and Lorenzo (the successive dedicatees of *The Prince*), Ippolito and Alessandro, to govern Florence under the tutelage of the Cardinal of Cortona. Cortona was dry, imperious and dilatory, and he fostered the haughty exclusiveness of his wards. Business of state flowed openly through the Medici palace, while the city's representatives had less and less say in their own affairs. Florence increasingly became a Roman dependency.

By the beginning of the following year, Machiavelli was compensated to some extent for the dispersal of the Oricellari circle by his admission to another group of *bons viveurs* and men of letters, centred this time on a wealthy commoner, Iacopo Falconetti, called Il Fornaciaio, after his foundry business (*fornace =* furnace). He had a garden outside the San Frediano gate, looking up to Bellosguardo, where he entertained his friends of all classes. The atmosphere was less intellectual than that of the Oricellari Gardens, less intense and not at all political. Food and song and entertainments were the fare he provided, and if Machiavelli, together with a girl singer with whose name, Barbera, his own was coupled for the rest of his life, was welcome there, it was as the author of *Mandragola* rather than of the *Discourses*. Towards the end of the year *Mandragola* was produced with great splendour and *éclat* at a house in Florence, and Falconetti, eager to rival its success, staged the same author's *Clizia* on January 13th, 1525. The scenery was painted by one of the artists who had been concerned with the rival production, Bastiano da Sangallo, and among the audience were the young Alessandro and Ippolito dei Medici. Pressed for time, Machiavelli had taken his

plot from the *Casina* of Plautus. He also followed the
Roman play fairly closely for something like one-fifth
of the text, but the effect of the play as a whole is completely his own. He broadened the human interest of
the situation by the introduction of new characters and
above all by setting it in a bourgeois Florentine background even more richly shaded than that of *Mandragola*. He took over two of the more successful songs
from that play, possibly at Barbera's instance, and
turned its recent success to good account by including
a reference to its principal characters in act two, scene
three.

A few weeks later, *The History of Florence* was
finished, emerging as the most personal and originally
conceived account of the city's history that had yet
been written. He showed himself far superior to his
sources, defter in his handling of narrative, quicker to
detect the likeliest course of cause and effect, shrewder
in his estimate of men's motives, yet, for all this, he did
not supplant them; his matter was too arbitrary, his
use of it too inaccurate. The long story was sustained
by a consistent vision of what had brought Florence
stage by stage from the break-up of the Roman Empire
to the present crisis, yet the general effect was lopsided
and uneven. This was due in part to his concentrating
on internal affairs up to the return of Cosimo from
exile in 1434 (the earlier histories which he used having
dwelled on external affairs), and external affairs thereafter (for fear of offending the present family by stressing their undermining the free constitution), and in
part to a determination that history should teach. It
taught best through events that were described in
detail, and this involved the crowding out of less rele-

vant episodes, even if from the point of view of a dispassionate, informed narrative, they had an important part to play. The effect is of an eccentric mask of events shaped over a concealed historical commentary.

The main themes are the old themes: the political divisions introduced and perpetuated by the papacy; the folly of relying on mercenaries; the decay of civic morale and—a topic given bitter emphasis—the fatal results of civic faction. But if the themes and the tone recall *The Prince*, there is no answering note of hopeful exhortation. The virtue of the Florentine citizen began to decline in the fourteenth century, when it became clear that class hatred between nobles and people had resulted not in levelling up but in levelling down, with the result that 'any clever law-maker could turn the government into whatever shape he pleased'. Such a man could at least protect his state from destruction from without, but after the death of Lorenzo the Magnificent, in the last words of the *History*, 'there sprang up those fatal seeds which, none knowing how to destroy them, brought, and still bring, ruin to Italy'.

In October of the previous year Francis I had once more invaded Italy in an attempt to break the double rule of Charles V in Lombardy and Naples. His army besieged Pavia throughout the winter, and month after month went by without the Imperial armies making a challenge. So notorious was their inaction that a pasquinade was published at Rome, offering a reward to any person who could find the Imperial army, lost in the month of October between France and Lombardy, and which had not been heard of since that time. But in February they were on the move and making contact with the French on the 24th, fought in the battle of Pavia what was perhaps the most sensational action of the wars of Italy. The French lost some eight thousand men; nearly every officer of rank was either slain or taken prisoner, and among the prisoners, the first ruling monarch to be captured in battle since the surrender of King John II at Poitiers, was Francis I himself.

After Pavia, a treaty was arranged whereby Florence and the papacy undertook to police Milan in return for Charles V's promise to protect the states of the Church and the Medici domains in Tuscany. It was published on May 1st, with the Viceroy of Naples signing on the Emperor's behalf. To smooth its ratification by Charles himself, Clement sent his nephew, Cardinal Salviati, as papal legate to Spain. Salviati had been the first man in Rome to whom Machiavelli had sent a copy of his *Art of War,* and in thanking him the cardinal had referred to his 'intelligence, experience, and good judgment'. Now, on the eve of leaving for Spain, he decided to take Machiavelli with him as his secretary, a choice that was endorsed by his father Iacopo, a man of great influence at the papal court, but disallowed by the Pope himself. The old stigma remained : Machiavelli could be indulged in a literary capacity or in affairs of a trifling nature, but he was to be kept away from political matters of importance. So three years after advising Raffaello Girolami on how to behave as an ambassador in Spain, Machiavelli was not trusted to go there as an ambassador's secretary.

It is doubtful if he was aware of Clement's veto; if he had been, he would hardly have gone to Rome in

May to present his history, nor is it likely that he would have pressed his view that a national militia should be raised in the states of the Church. Clement, indeed, not only rewarded him for *The History of Florence* but listened to his plan for a papal militia. Machiavelli had remained convinced that national troops were the only answer to Italy's wars since his first years in the Florentine service. His aim was to provide a loyal papal army in central Italy and it found powerful supporters, as a result of whose representations, Machiavelli was sent to Faenza to talk over the practical implications of the scheme with Guicciardini, who was warned of his coming by a papal brief which announced : 'This is an important matter, and on it depends the salvation of the states of the Church, as well as of Italy itself, and, almost, of the whole of Christendom.' Machiavelli arrived on June 19th and found Guicciardini sympathetic but not in favour of acting on it at once. Clement had liked the scheme for its cheapness, but it would in fact mean more money than could be raised locally, and as Guicciardini candidly pointed out in a letter to the Pope, 'This enterprise would need to be founded on the love of the people, and the people of the Romagna have not the slightest love for the Church. There is no security here for either life or property, and as a result men look to foreign princes, on whom everyone in this province depends. And to hope to compose the militia, as Machiavelli suggests, of men independent of either faction [French or Imperial] would be equal to composing it of none.' After this it was not perhaps altogether ingenuously that he continued : 'Nevertheless, if the thing is to be attempted at all risks, I will throw myself into it heart and soul.'

To all this Clement made no reply. His enthusiasm had cooled. Machiavelli waited until the end of July, and when it was clear that his experience was not going to be called on to save the Papal States let alone 'the whole of Christendom', he went back to Florence.

The long sojourn in Faenza had not been fruitless, however. It increased the sympathy between the two men, and the greater part of Machiavelli's correspondence from now on consists of letters to and from Guicciardini. It came to have much in common with the letters to Vettori in 1513–15, a blend of gossip and banter, politics and pure literary artifice, and took place against a background of deepening gloom. Charles V was supreme in Milan and Naples, but there was no reason to assume that he would be content with domains separated by the hostile zone of Tuscany and the Papal States. With Francis a prisoner, there was no one for Florence to appeal to. The Pope treated her as a Roman dependency and was himself irresolute and short of money and men. Venice was not to be trusted. The only hope seemed to lie in an attempt made by the French regent, Louise of Savoy, to find a pro-French party in Italy. The negotiations for this forlorn hope were conducted by Girolamo Morone, secretary to the exiled Duke of Milan, Francesco Sforza, and he offered the leadership of Italian resistance to the Marquis of Pescara in return for the crown of Naples, stressing not only the personal advantage he would gain from this but also the glory he would gain from being the liberator of his country. Pescara, though sworn to secrecy, believed the plot had little hope of success and revealed it to Charles V. On October 15th Morone was seized and imprisoned.

This news provoked from Machiavelli a letter to Guicciardini which was a hectic mixture of grief, impatience and bravado. 'Morone has been seized, and the duchy of Milan is done for, and just as that man waited to be snuffed out, so will all the other princes wait, nor is there any hope of mending matters.' Then, a few lines later, referring to a project to perform *Mandragola* at Faenza: 'Let us have a merry carnival, and engage a lodging for Barbera among the friars, and if they do not lose their heads I will not take any payment, and recommend me to La Maliscotta [a courtesan he had met at Faenza in June] and let me know how the arrangements for the comedy are going on, and when you intend to have it played. I have had that increase of one hundred ducats for my *History*. Now I am beginning to write again, and vent my rage by accusing the princes who have all done everything to bring us to this pass.' The letter was signed 'Niccolò Machiavelli, *istorico, Comico et Tragico*'.

Though dark portents obscured the international scene, 1525 had been a year of promise and release for Machiavelli. He had been disappointed by the failure of his militia scheme, but at least it had brought him back into the world of affairs again. Clement had liked *The History of Florence*, and his salary had been raised as a result. The sumptuous performance of *Clizia* in January had spread his fame as a dramatist, and in February *Mandragola* was given in Venice—and had a flattering reception, as another company was giving a translation of the *Menaechmi* of Plautus at the same time, and though this famous play was performed by a good company, it was held to be 'a dead thing' in comparison with Machiavelli's. In August he went to

Venice himself, employed by the wool guild to settle a trade dispute which arose from the ill-treatment of some Florentine merchants. According to rumours filtering back to Florence, he won two or three thousand ducats in a lottery there, and Nerli wrote to congratulate him, saying that his friends were all delighted by the news—'and it seems to them that what men have failed to provide for your merits has been provided by chance'. His letters towards the end of 1525 contain gaiety as well as wit, notably an undated one in which he explained to Guicciardini, in terms of burlesque philological and antiquarian scholarship, two proverbial Florentine expressions used in *Mandragola*. As Guicciardini said in his last letter of the year—'recreation is more necessary than ever in these times of crisis'. When carnival time came, however, and Machiavelli was to have been listening to Barbera as she sang the interludes between the acts, Guicciardini had to be in Rome discussing the consequences of the treaty of Madrid with Clement, and the performance was cancelled.

By this treaty, Charles released Francis from captivity on the assurance that he would make no attempt to recover France's lost power in Italy. A year of suspense was over : some sort of action would surely follow, and it seemed likely that the Italian states would be the losers either way. Francis I would almost certainly break an oath extorted under duress and enter Italy again ; there were ominous signs that, even if he did not, the Imperialists did not feel secure in Italy and would try to extend their rule. Machiavelli wrote a letter to Filippo Strozzi on March 10th 1526, which was shown to Clement, and another on the 15th to Guicciardini in Rome on the same theme. 'I think,' it ran, 'that however things turn out, there must be war, and soon, in Italy.' One thing above all must be avoided : a reliance on money rather than arms. 'We must make some resistance, concealed or open, or we shall wake up one morning to find it all over. I will say something which will seem mad to you, and suggest a plan which will seem rash or ridiculous ; nevertheless, these times demand decisions that are bold, unconventional and strange.' And he went on to suggest that Giovanni delle Bande Nere should be given an Italian army to show that the Italian states were prepared to defend themselves from any foe—French or Imperial. He was a fine soldier and the best leader available in Italy— 'brave, impetuous, with grand ideas, and able to appreciate great causes'. The letter ended with a characteristic change of key. 'Barbera is there ; if you can be of any service to her, I commend her to you, for she is of much greater concern to me than is the Emperor.' The suggestion about Giovanni came to nothing ; Clement declined to do anything so provocative and expensive.

In Florence, a thorough reappraisal of the city's fortifications was made for the first time since 1494. Five procurators of the walls were appointed in May, at Machiavelli's suggestion, and he was made their chancellor. But before this, early in April, he had already accompanied the veteran engineer Pietro Navarra on a tour of the walls, of which he gave an account in a report to Clement written immediately afterwards. He described how they had walked along every stretch of the walls, and gave point by point their opinions ; for the most part they were attributed to Navarra, but this was possibly in part a following of his own advice to Raffaello Girolami.

From tower to tower, from gate to gate, it was the same story : the existing structures must be made lower and more massive, and better armed. Great bastions and solid gun platforms were becoming the rule in modern fortification, and Florence badly needed them. Nothing fancy, no intricate design to provide flanking cover for every yard of exposed wall, but squat walls and platforms to support a weight of fire sufficient to keep the enemy at a distance ; Florence should aim at out-gunning any possible attack. They picked their way across the fields belonging to citizens whose houses crowded against the walls, looking up at the walls and across to the slopes and hills that commanded them, judging a section at a time. There were old walls to be repaired and others to be re-sited. But most important of all was their opinion that the San Miniato district was indefensible and should be left outside the newly strengthened city circuit, although this meant leaving it at the mercy of an enemy. They agreed, reluctantly, that this was essential; it should be abandoned, even destroyed, to prevent an enemy establishing a foothold there. Clement refused to accept this, and Machiavelli was forced to appeal to Guicciardini to use his influence ; he went so far as to write three times to him in one day on the subject, pointing out the work and expense that would be involved if San Miniato were to be included, and the alarming effect this extra tract of vulnerable wall would have on the defenders. The Pope continued to object, the work was held up, and when the danger of invasion really became grave, in the following year, Florence was still unprepared to meet it.

In May came the first move to reintroduce the French into Italy. On the 22nd the treaty of Cognac was published, whereby Clement absolved Francis from any promise he had made to Charles V during his imprisonment. France was to free Naples, and to restore Francesco Sforza in Milan under French protection. The forces of the League thus created between the Pope, Venice and Francis I were under the command of the Duke of Urbino, Francesco Maria della Rovere, and it turned out to be a disastrous appointment, his irresolution and lack of grip leading to widespread alarm and depression on the part of the League's supporters. In June Machiavelli was sent to the League's army in Lombardy to consult with Guicciardini about the position of Florence—the Signoria thinking that he could best represent how unprepared they were to face a siege, and knowing that he was on terms of friendship with the one man in Clement's service they could really trust.

While he was away he had a cheerful letter from Iacopo Falconetti saying that Barbera was missing him, and a bitter one from Vettori, who was also in Florence, reporting the miserable failure of a papal attack on Siena, designed to stabilize its government in the interests of the League. He reflects a widespread sense of hopelessness. 'You know', he wrote on August 5th, 'that I very grudgingly believe in anything supernatural; but this rout seems to me as extraordinary, I don't say miraculous, as anything that has happened since '94; it seems indeed like certain episodes I have read about in the Bible, when fear entered into men and they fled, and they did not know from whom.' His general opinion of the striking power of the League's armies was that they could not even force their way into an oven. And between Machiavelli and Vettori sprang up a late version of the 'peace' correspondence, though now it was in terms of strategy. Machiavelli, as usual, being for action : attack on Genoa, attack on Naples; Vettori being more cautious and cynical. For all that, he passed Machiavelli's letters on to Clement's counsellor Filippo Strozzi, though they cannot be said to have made any impression there.

The League was besieging Cremona, and as no progress appeared to be made, Machiavelli was sent from headquarters by Guicciardini to report on the situation there. But Vettori's 'oven' was an exaggeration; the city surrendered to the League on September 2nd almost as soon as he arrived and they were now free to proceed in strength against Milan and Genoa. The orders they received, however, were not to advance, but to withdraw south of the Po.

This galling news was the result of disturbances in Rome. During the siege of Cremona, Clement had been having trouble with his rivals, the Colonna, whose troops, encouraged by Charles V's agent at Rome, Don Ugo da Moncada, had been marauding in the countryside about the city until Clement negotiated a truce with them. He at once took advantage of this to disband his own troops, it being his habit to economize whenever possible. The folly of this action was soon seen. Three days before Cremona fell, the Colonna entered Rome with their troops and sacked the Vatican and St. Peter's, looting what valuables they could lay hands on and forcing Clement to shut himself up in

Castel S. Angelo, the papal fortress near the Vatican. Moncada was then able to negotiate openly and from strength with the Pope, and it was as a result of this that the League forces were checked till truce conditions had been worked out. After extorting terms from Clement, Moncada and the Colonna captains dropped on their knees and begged his absolution for what they had just done. According to Nardi, Clement had enough spirit of his own to comment *ave rex Iudeorum, et dabant ei alapas,*[1] and enough spirit of the times to wait only till their backs were turned before sending an army to ravage the Colonna estates and attack Naples.

Guicciardini had fallen back to Piacenza, and Machiavelli went with him, writing in early October an analysis of the present situation and its causes in a letter to Bartolomeo Cavalcanti, one of the most brilliant of the younger generation of Florentines, with whom he had struck up a close friendship in the last few years. He girded at the recent long-drawn-out siege of Cremona, 'which ran counter to the rule [his own rule : *vide Discourses,* Book One, Chapter 23] which says : it is dangerous to stake your whole fortune without using your whole strength', and criticized the Pope for being miserly and for allowing himself to be taken 'like an infant'. When the truce was announced he returned to Florence, but on November 30th the Signoria sent him back to Guicciardini, then at Modena, to stress the weak condition of Florence and her need of protection by papal troops. The Florentines, at the mercy of policies decided on in Rome, felt

[1] John 19.3. 'The soldiers . . . said, Hail, King of the Jews ! and they smote him with their hands.'

isolated and helpless, and increasingly disinclined to trust the motives of the cardinal of Cortona. Machiavelli was urged to beg Guicciardini's opinion of events, and to find out 'whether he, like ourselves, despairs of our safety'. Guicciardini was too aware of the confused state of the League's resources to offer any reassurance, and Machiavelli came back without cheer, and slowly, making the wintry crossing of the Apennines in stages, for by this December he was feeling his age.

During the winter the Imperial forces slowly grew and consolidated. They crossed the Po, while the League's remained passive. Florence was fearful that at the first break in the weather the enemy, already said to be swearing 'by the glorious sack of Florence', would strike at them. Unable to abide the tension, they sent Machiavelli again to Guicciardini, who was then at Parma, on February 3rd, 1527, to point out once more the weakness of Florence's defences and to beg for military aid. This time he did not return at once, but stayed with Guicciardini as the League forces slowly gave ground during the next agonizing months; from Parma they shifted down to Bologna, from Bologna to Imola, from Imola to Forlì and to Brisighella. During all these stages the Duke of Urbino remained so inactive that he was rumoured to have accepted bribes from the enemy. From March, Clement fatally believed that he was covered by a truce signed with Charles de Lannoy, the Imperial Viceroy of Naples, who had been anxious in that way to put a stop to the Pope's attack on Naples. This truce was intended to be binding on all Imperial forces in Italy, but Bourbon, who commanded in the north, was no longer able to control his own men, avid as they were for the spoils of Florence and Rome, and their slow pressure south continued through the stormy spring.

During his negotiations with Lannoy, Clement had promised that Florence would pay sixty thousand ducats over to Bourbon, and Machiavelli, suspecting that Florence, however desperate her position, would haggle over this payment in her usual manner, wrote a dispatch from Bologna on March 23rd to urge them to be quick : even if the truce fell through, he pointed out, they would still have to raise the money to defend themselves; 'in either one case or the other it would give us time, and if ever the proverb was true that "to have time is to have life", it is in this case most decidedly so'. and when the truce was seen to be a dead letter as regards the northern theatre of war, he continued to offer advice—that they should bribe the Venetians to aid them, for instance—with a freedom he had never before shown in his relations with his superiors. Indeed, the circumstances of his employment hardly resembled those of the years 1498–1512. He was more of a free-lance. In some respects he was used by Guicciardini as he had been by Soderini, as a man of integrity and intelligence who could function more effectively in many situations than the officials directly responsible. This friendship with Guicciardini put him on a different plane from an ordinary diplomatic agent, and the divided nature of the Florentine government, where the city's interests had to be pressed half-surreptitiously past the wider interests of the Medici family, made his link with the Signoria a more personal one than it had been in his former diplomatic career.

The situation was not without gleams of hope. The Imperial forces were scattered over a vast area of land which was now snow-bound, now water-logged, and were in a surly mood which on at least one occasion—when the great George von Frundsberg was infuriated into a fatal heart attack by his own men's insubordination—broke into open mutiny. Machiavelli even wrote to the Signoria from Forlì on April 13th of the Imperial forces : 'They remain at the present like those bands of adventurers which, for a hundred and fifty years have gone roaming through the country, levying tribute, or ravaging it, without ever capturing any place.' Less than a month later these same adventurers were to capture Rome itself. But his mood was generally clouded by dread. No one knew which way the enemy would move when they shook themselves out of winter quarters in good earnest. His heart bled for Florence and for Guicciardini, both forced to wait, caught between an enemy which had not declared his aims and a leader, Clement, who appeared to have none to declare. On April 18th, writing from Brisighella the last letter he ever wrote to Vettori, he raged against the wavering that doomed a situation in which decisions should be made *subito, subito*.

The danger to Florence was brought all the nearer by letters from his family. His second son, Lodovico, was away trading in the Levant, but the eldest, Bernardo was there, working for the procurators of the walls, and so were the others, Guido, Piero, his daughter Bartolomea (La Baccina), and the infant Totto, who was still a babe in arms. He wrote to Guido, intended for the Church but still a young schoolboy, on April 2nd from Imola :

'Guido, my dearest son, I have had a letter from you which has given me the greatest pleasure, especially as you say you are quite recovered—I could not have better news than that; and if God grant you—and me —life I think we shall make you a man of good standing, if you are prepared to play your part. For among the influential friends I already have, I have struck up a new friendship with Cardinal Cibo [papal legate and cousin of Clement; Machiavelli had met him recently at Bologna], so much that I am surprised at it myself; and this will serve you in good stead. But you must study and, since you no longer have the excuse of illness, work hard at your books and at music, for you see what honour my own little learning brings me. So, my son, if you want to please me and bring profit and credit to yourself, work with a will, for if you help yourself, others will help you.'

He went on to talk about a mule that had been causing trouble, and ended

'Greet Mona Marietta, and tell her that I have been on the point of leaving day after day, and still am, and I have never longed so much to be in Florence as I do now, but I can do nothing about it. Simply tell her that, whatever she hears, she can rely on my being there before any trouble starts. Kiss Baccina, Piero, and Totto. . . . Be happy. . . . Christ keep you all.'

Guido's reply, sent on April 17th, shows how much the family was comforted by Machiavelli's promise to be home before danger was imminent. They had been bringing supplies into Florence from the villa, he said, preparing for siege, but they had no more fear of the 'Lanziginec' [the German *Lanzknechts*] now their father was coming home. He arrived on April 22nd. The Imperial army was already on the move. On April 26th Bourbon himself was within twenty miles of the city. It is true that a League force reached Barberino, only twenty miles away, on the same day, and that the Duke of Urbino, with a force of eleven thousand Venetian troops, was at about the same distance, but as Machiavelli had warned Vettori on the 18th, the League's soldiers were hardly preferable to the Imperial troops. They were not interested in a settlement; 'those who relish war, as these soldiers do, would be mad if they praised peace'.

There had indeed been strong pressure put on the Signoria to arm the citizens, a pressure resisted because Cortona was known to be opposed to anything so potentially explosive, but on that same April 26th a violent demonstration in the Piazza della Signoria coincided with the news that the Cardinal with his advisers and the young Ippolito dei Medici had fled the city. In fact they had only gone to greet the allied commanders, but the most stridently anti-Medicean element in the crowd insisted on the proclamation of a republic, and, under menaces, the Signoria agreed. The popular triumph was short-lived. Cortona was only two miles outside the gates when the news reached him, and he at once turned back with the large escort of horsemen. The effect of their appearance in the approaches to the piazza, and the sound of their arquebuses fired into the air, changed the mood of the demonstrators so abruptly that, as one observer put it, mouths that opened to say 'Popolo!' shouted 'Palle!' instead. Having cleared the piazza the troops began to force the doors of the Palazzo Vecchio, until Iacopo

Nardi, Machiavelli's historian associate of the Oricellari Gardens, organized the hurling down of stones
kept on the roof for such emergencies. The troops
drew off, but not before one stone had knocked an
arm off Michelangelo's David which stood below,
breaking it in two places. The repulse was clearly only
a temporary one: Cortona had the overwhelming
advantage of arms and was prepared to use it. Guicciardini, who had come in from the League camp in
the Cardinal's wake, persuaded him to negotiate
instead, and wrote out the terms—full pardon for full
surrender—there and then on the counter of a neigh-
bouring shop. Inside the Palazzo they were amended
by Vettori, who had been one of the defenders, and
were then accepted by both sides. The rebels were
allowed to go to their homes and their recent proceedings declared null. *Il tumulto del Venerdì,* as the events
of this Friday came to be known, had been little more
than a storm in a tea-cup, but it was also a dress-
rehearsal for the full-scale revolution that was almost
bound to come if the League suffered any reverse.
Botched as it had been, the tumult had shown how
much antagonism there was to the Medicean régime
within the city, and the exiles of 1522, including Zanobi
Buondelmonti and Battista della Palla, had gained the
support of Filippo Strozzi, and were actively seeking
armed assistance without. The chief supporters of the
Medici were largely influenced by the financial advantages of the link with Medicean Rome: if that were to
break, a major cause of their loyalty would snap as
well.

Machiavelli had been in Florence on the 26th, but
he is not known to have taken any part in the rising,

and indeed, although so many of his friends were concerned, it is not easy to guess where his sympathies
would have lain : with the mob outside the Palazzo
chanting their demands to be given arms; with Vettori,
Nardi and Luigi Guicciardini (Francesco's brother)
within, forced into making gestures without knowing
how far they would be echoed by events; with Guicciardini and the League party, who were mainly concerned with the defence of central Italy as a whole; or
with Buondelmonti and the exiles who were prepared
to use Bourbon and his Imperialist troops to turn the
Medici out of Florence.

A few days later, early in May, he left with Guicciardini. The Imperialists had swung past Florence
to avoid the League's covering force, and were making
for Rome; the army of the League followed slowly
and uselessly after. On May 6th Bourbon attacked the
virtually defenceless papal city and though he was
killed (Benvenuto Cellini claimed to have shot him) his
troops broke in and sacked it, while Clement took
refuge again in Castel S. Angelo. The Imperial troops,
without effective leadership, starved of pay, voracious
for self-indulgence after a long winter of abstinence
and, in the case of the Protestant contingent, filled with
a nun-raping, priest-baiting, church-stripping fervour,
caused so much havoc in and around the city that it
was some days before reliable news got back to
Florence. When it did, the last props slid from under
Cortona's rule. Unpopular and inefficient, clearly incapable of reform, and deprived now of the prestige
and wealth of Rome, the régime collapsed. The opposition was no longer unprepared. On May 16th the

Republic was restored; on the 17th the Medici left the city.

Machiavelli heard of the change of government at Civitavecchia, where he had been sent by Guicciardini to see Andrea Doria, admiral of the papal fleet, to find out what plans there were to rescue Clement and help him escape from Rome. He reported to Guicciardini that Doria could only act if Clement were brought down to the coast. Then he turned north to Florence, hoping that in the city, returning day by day to its pre-1512 framework, there would be a place for him once more. The Great Council was restored—and literally reopened, as the walls inserted to make quarters for the Medicean guard were demolished. The Ten of War was restored. But his own position was uncertain. Once more revolution caught him on the wrong side; as in 1512 he had been identified with Soderini, now he was associated with the Medici, and though others, like Vettori and Strozzi, who had been associated with them far more closely, were accepted by the Republic, he had neither wealth nor a great name to help him cross from one camp to the other; after even the most enlightened revolution, desert is only one of the factors that determine the allocation of offices.

His age, too, was against him; he was fifty-eight. And his health was probably failing: he had felt the need for some time to take mild drugs for a digestive complaint, and the last months, involving a good deal of travelling in hard weather, had not helped. And, more important still, the new government was Savonarolist in temper and he was known not to be that sort of republican. He had originally come to office in a wave of anti-Savonarolist feeling; it was under a Savonarolist successor of Soderini, Ridolfi, that he had first been cold-shouldered. And if he had preached republicanism in the *Discourses* and his advice to Leo and Giulio, it had always been republicanism at the convenience of the Medici.

However, the office of secretary to the newly re-formed Ten was vacant. Machiavelli had filled it well before, and he had only recently been in charge of work that came within its purview, the strengthening of the walls, and the problem of defence was now more crucial than ever. His candidacy was supported by his old Oricellari friends Buondelmonti and Alamanni. But on June 10th the position went to the ex-secretary of the *Otto di Pratica,* the Medicean equivalent of the Ten. It was the rebuff final. Ten days later he became ill. It was the old stomach trouble, but in a seriously worse form. On June 21st, after making his confession, he died, surrounded by his family and friends.

If the trouble was, as is most likely, an ulcer, then the various distresses and fatigues of the last months would easily account for his death in late middle age, and it would be sentimental to stress the anguish of the last weeks when he was left outside the new government which included so many of his friends and his ideals. We see the last Florentine Republic in the blaze of light reflected from its magnificent struggle until 1530 to keep itself free. In June 1527 it had still to prove itself, and it still incorporated much that was left over from the previous régime. Machiavelli was too sardonic, and in personal matters too much a realist, to see his failure to get the secretaryship as a specially cruel blow. It was a long shot, and it had not come off.

If it did increase his worries, it was in a practical way; he had a wife and the four younger children to provide for, and he had no employment. He was taken ill at a time when Florence had been saved at Rome's expense, but, it must have seemed, only for a while, with every hand ready to be raised against her, with no defence apart from walls which were unfinished and citizens who had neither been refined by the firm rule of a wise prince, inspired by a revitalized religion, nor disciplined by arms. How would this turn out?—that question, and not, Why is Fortune so cruel as to give my job to another man? must have been uppermost in Machiavelli's mind in his last days.

On June 22nd he was buried in Santa Croce.

Appendix: Machiavelli's Works; Their Dates, and the Italian Titles of Works Referred to in English in the Text

Italian title	Referred to in text and index as:	Date of composition (Dates in square brackets are conjectural)
Discorso della guerra di Pisa	Report on the Pisan War	1499
Descrizione del modo tenuto dal Duca Valentino nell' ammazzare Vitellozzo Vitelli, Oliverotto da Fermo, il signor Pagolo e il Duca di Gravina Orsini	Description of the Manner in which Duke Valentino put Vitellozzo Vitelli . . . etc. . . . to death	1503
Parole sopra la provvisione del danaio	Remarks on the raising of money	1503
Del modo di trattare i sudditi della Valdichiana ribellati	On the Method of dealing with the Rebels of the Val di Chiana	1503
Decennale Primo	The First Decade	1504
Discorso dell'ordinare lo stato di Firenze alle armi	Discourse on Florentine military preparation	1506
Rapporto delle cose dell' Alemagna	Report on Germany	1508
Discorso sopra le cose della Magna e sopra lo imperatore	Discourse on Germany and the Emperor	1509
Decennale Secondo	The Second Decade	[1509]
Ritratto delle cose della Magna	Description of German Affairs	[after April, 1512]
Ritratto delle cose di Francia	Description of French Affairs	[after April, 1512 and before August, 1513]
Il Principe	The Prince	1513
Discorsi sopra la prima deca di Tito Livio	Discourses on the First Decade of Livy	1515–16–17
Discorso o dialogo intorno alla nostra lingua	Discourse or Dialogue on our Language	[conventionally 1514 but probably later]
L'Asino d'oro	The Golden Ass	[1517 or 18]

Mandragola	Mandragola	1518
Belfagor	Belfagor	[1515–1520]
Dell' Arte della Guerra	The Art of War	1519–20
Sommario delle cose della città di Lucca	Summary of Lucchese Affairs	1520
La vita di Castruccio Castracani da Lucca	The Life of Castruccio Castracani of Lucca	1520
Discorso delle cose fiorentine dopo la morte di Lorenzo	Discourse on Florentine affairs after the Death of Lorenzo	1519 or 1520
Istorie Fiorentine	The History of Florence	Begun 1520 finished 1525
Memoriale a Raffaello Girolami	Advice to Raffaello Girolami	1522
Clizia	Clizia	[1524–5]
Relazione di una visita fatta per fortificare Firenze	Report on the Fortifications of Florence	1526

Note. In addition to the poems listed above, Machiavelli wrote a number of shorter ones. The chronology of several of these remains obscure.

Bibliography

MACHIAVELLI'S WORKS

The most convenient edition of Machiavelli's works in Italian is the one volume, *Tutte le Opere Storiche e letterarie di Niccolò Machiavelli*, edited by Guido Mazzoni and Mario Casella, but it should be noted that, in spite of the title, some important minor political works are omitted. These can be found in volume 2 of Niccolò Machiavelli, *Opere*, edited by Antonio Panella. The *Lettere Familiari*, consisting of private letters to and from Machiavelli have been printed (with foolish expurgations) by Edoardo Alvisi. A more convenient edition, without cuts, is *Lettere di Niccolò Machiavelli*, 2 vols., 1915, with a preface by Giovanni Papini. A collection of official letters is to be found in *Scritti Inediti di Niccolò Machiavelli risguardanti la Storia e la Milizia (1499–1512)*, edited by Giuseppe Canestrini, 1857.

TRANSLATIONS

The Historical, Political, and Diplomatic Writings of Niccolò Machiavelli, translated by Christian E. Detmold, Boston, 4 vols., 1891, is the most useful *corpus* of Machiavelli's works in translation. A new one has been promised by Allan H. Gilbert. There is a new translation of *The Prince* by George Bull in Penguin Books, 1959; of *Mandragola, Clizia, Bel-*

fagor, etc., in *The Literary Works of Niccolò Machiavelli*, by J. R. Hale, 1960, which also includes a selection from the private correspondence.

BIOGRAPHIES

The best is Roberto Ridolfi, *Vita di Niccolò Machiavelli*, Rome, 1954, but the rambling *Life and Times of Niccolò Machiavelli* by P. Villari (first English edition, 1878–83), remains the most useful Life available in English, though the translations from Machiavelli's own works are sometimes shortened or altered without warning. The edition of *The Prince*, by L. A. Burd (Oxford, 1891), contains an invaluable 'Historical Abstract', fitting Machiavelli's works and movements into a chronological table of events.

CRITICAL WORKS

From a vast literature I mention three books, all available and in English. Most forceful and suggestive is J. H. Whitfield, *Machiavelli*, 1947. Herbert Butterfield's *The Statecraft of Machiavelli*, 1940 (reprinted in 1955), provides an elegantly neo-Elizabethan assault on Machiavelli. In *Machiavelli and the Renaissance*, 1958, Federico Chabod reprints some of the articles which have made him the doyen of Machiavelli studies in Italy.

BIBLIOGRAPHY

Il Principio della Forza nel Pensiero Politico di Niccolò Machiavelli, by Achille Norsa, Milan, 1936, contains a classified bibliography of works relating to Machiavelli which lists over 2,000 items. Subsequent work can be traced in P. H. Harris, 'Progress in Machiavelli Studies', *Italica*, March 1941, and thenceforward in the annual bibliographies of Renaissance studies published in *Italian Studies* and *Studies in Philology*.

BACKGROUND

Garrett Mattingly's *Renaissance Diplomacy*, 1955, provides an admirable account of the methods used by diplomatic agents and the role they played in the political life of the age.

Index

(Italic numbers indicate Machiavelli's opinion.)